Climbing towards
Stórasúla (Stage 3a)

KNIFE
EDGE
Outdoor Guidebooks

AF292532

Publisher: Knife Edge Outdoor Limited (NI648568)
12 Torrent Business Centre, Donaghmore, County Tyrone, BT70 3BF, UK
www.knifeedgeoutdoor.com

©Andrew McCluggage 2023
All photographs: ©Andrew McCluggage 2023
ISBN: 978-1-912933-16-7

First edition 2023

A catalogue record for this book is available from the British Library.

Mapping produced by Knife Edge Outdoor Limited: ©Knife Edge Outdoor Limited 2023.

Map data: ©OpenStreetMap contributors. Data available under the Open Data Commons Open Database License (ODbL). Also contains data from the IS 50V and ÍslandsDEM databases of the Land Survey of Iceland (Landmælingar Íslands) from 10/2022.

Front cover: The 'Rainbow Mountains' near Landmannalaugar (Stage 1)
Title page: Contrasting colours on Stage 1
This page: Climbing above the Ljósá River (Stage 4a)
Back cover: Hiking towards Stórasúla (Stage 3a)
Back cover flap: Views of Eyjafjallajökull (Stage 4a)

All routes described in this book have been recently walked by the author and both the author and publisher have made all reasonable efforts to ensure that all information is as accurate as possible. However, while a printed book remains constant for the life of an edition, things in the countryside often change. Trails are subject to forces outside our control. For example, landslides, tree-falls or other matters can result in damage to paths or route changes; waymarks and signposts may fade or be destroyed by wind, snow or the passage of time; or trails may not be maintained by the relevant authorities. If you notice any discrepancies between the contents of this guide and the facts on the ground, then please let us know. Our contact details are listed at the back of this book.

Contents

*The wondeful view from the S rim
of the Torfajökull Caldera (Stage 2)*

Getting Help

Emergency services number: dial 112

Distress signal

The signal that you are in distress is 6 blasts on a whistle spaced over a minute, followed by a minute's silence. Then repeat. The acknowledgment that your signal has been received is 3 blasts of a whistle over a minute followed by a minute's silence. At night, flashes of a torch can also be used in the same sequences. Always carry a torch and whistle.

Signalling to a helicopter from the ground

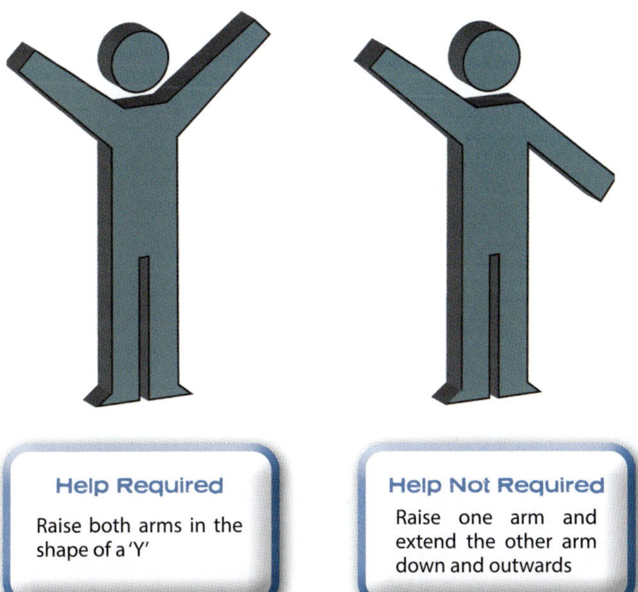

Help Required

Raise both arms in the shape of a 'Y'

Help Not Required

Raise one arm and extend the other arm down and outwards

WARNING

Hills, cliffs and mountains can be dangerous places and walking is a potentially dangerous activity. Some of the routes described in this guide cross potentially hazardous terrain. You walk entirely at your own risk. It is solely your responsibility to ensure that you and all members of your group have adequate experience, fitness and equipment. Neither the author nor the publisher accepts any responsibility or liability whatsoever for death, injury, loss, damage or inconvenience resulting from use of this book, participation in the activity of mountain walking or otherwise.

Some land may be privately owned so we cannot guarantee that there is a legal right of entry to the land. Occasionally, routes change as a result of land disputes.

The basalt deserts of Stage 3b

Introduction

It is no exaggeration to state that Iceland, the 'Land of Fire and Ice', is completely and utterly unlike any other place on earth. Volcanoes are responsible for the 'fire' part of this nickname because the island is littered with them: incredibly, more than 30 of Iceland's 130 volcanoes are active or dormant (meaning that they may erupt in the future) and some of them still erupt regularly. The 'ice' part of the nickname refers to Iceland's glaciers which cover a huge 11% of the country's surface area. The existence of so many active volcanoes and so many glaciers on a single island is extraordinary in itself but in Iceland, 'fire' and 'ice' actually coexist, with the glaciers often covering the active volcanoes. Although this is a relatively uncommon phenomenon, it is one that you will witness daily on the Laugavegur Trail (LT) and its southern extension, the Fimmvörðuháls Trail (FT): incredibly, they lead the trekker right into the heart of Iceland's unique and exhilarating ice-capped volcanic terrain. From start to finish, you will be astounded by the unusual, starkly beautiful and constantly changing landscapes, the likes of which you will not find anywhere else on the planet.

The volcanic activity has a profound impact on the personality of the trek. The impressive volcanic peaks and ridges are an almost constant companion and seemingly everywhere, there is evidence of past eruptions. You will walk across old lava flows, immense ash-fields and ground strewn with volcanic rock bombs. Incredibly, you will spend almost two days walking through the middle of one of the world's few super-volcanoes (Torfajökull) where, right beside the path, steam gushes out of the ground, hissing loudly, and water boils visibly on the surface. And you can spend the night on the slopes of Eyjafjallajökull which famously erupted in 2010, grounding airplanes all over Europe.

Visually, the scenery is unconventional, inconceivable and totally awe-inspiring. Clear paths and tracks lead you along spectacular ridges, across high mountain passes and through spectacular valleys and plains. Day by day, the terrain changes and surprising new landscapes are displayed. At the northern end of the LT, you will find the 'Rainbow

Mountains' which are spectacularly multi-coloured: a beguiling and vibrant mix of orange, yellow and pink which contrasts sublimely with the bright white snow patches which lie long into the trekking season. In the middle of the trek, the jagged peaks and ridges are less colourful but equally striking: seemingly everywhere, the monochrome basalt rock has been delicately frosted with moss of an otherworldly shade of green. To the S of the LT, closer to Þórsmörk, the landscape is softer and warmer with flat-topped cliffs and ridges which support more vegetation: Katla and Eyjafjallajökull, two huge ice-capped volcanoes, form the backdrop. Even further S, on the FT, the vegetation thickens and you traverse knife-edged ridges across magnificent slopes of the deepest green. Then, near the Fimmvörðuháls pass, you will witness the dark lava flows, craters and ash-fields produced by the Eyjafjallajökull eruption. Finally, on the path along the Skógá River, you are treated to one of the finest collections of waterfalls in the world. In summary, it is fair to say that the quality and variety of the views on offer are staggering.

With such amazing sights to experience, it is hardly surprising that the LT and FT are popular treks. However, although you will share the trail with others, the quantity of hikers is rarely oppressive. The fact that each hut has a finite number of beds imposes a drag on the number of trekkers: the number of campers is unrestricted but not everyone wants to carry heavy camping gear. Although there can be many day-walkers around Landmannalaugar, Þórsmörk and Skógar (which are served by buses), the vast landscape is easily large enough to swallow them and most do not delve too far into the interior. Get a reasonably early start and you will find yourself largely alone for much of the day. You will occasionally pass, or be passed by, other trekkers but, for most people, these fleeting interactions are no bad thing. At night, you will camp out or stay in one of the mountain huts. Although the facilities are basic, the huts and campsites are magnificently situated in the wild and remote terrain: there you will meet many of the people that you passed earlier in the day, making it easy to develop trail friendships. The LT is a sociable trek and some of the bonds forged can last a lifetime.

In short, the LT and FT are two of the most unique and rewarding treks in the world. There is a clear sense of wilderness and adventure. Those who walk these trails witness wild and spectacular scenery which is accessible to very few. Some people are happy to hike only the LT, perhaps leaving the FT for a future trip. Others attempt only the FT because it can be completed in one long day. However, for the most complete experience, we prefer to link the two treks. Whichever option you choose, the experience will be unforgettable.

The LT is 56km (35 miles) long with 1700-2100m (5600-6800ft) of ascent/descent (depending on direction of travel). The FT is 28km (17 miles) long with 1100-1300m (3700-4400ft) of ascent/descent (depending on direction of travel). When combined, they are 84km (52 miles) long with 2800-3400m (9300-11200ft) of ascent/descent (depending on direction of travel). Those statistics may sound intimidating but it is reassuring to note that many thousands of normal people complete the trails each year: with the right preparation, planning and approach, they are manageable for most people of reasonable fitness. Yes, it is a challenge but it is an achievable one. And that is where this book comes in: most of what you need to know to plan, and prepare for, the LT/FT is here within these pages and the entire route is described in detail to guide you on the trail itself. Furthermore, unlike some other books, this one contains real maps: for each stage, there are 1:40,000 scale maps to go with the accurate and concise route descriptions. Because we were unable to find commercially available maps with sufficient detail for our purposes, we commissioned our own maps: we believe that these are the finest maps available for the LT/FT. As well as including these maps in this book, we have also published a sheet map for the LT/FT which is extremely helpful for planning and navigation: *'The Laugavegur Trail & the Fimmvörðuháls Trail'* (ISBN: 9781912933501).

We aim to ensure that you have the best chance possible of completing the trek. We place great importance on the correct preparation and we focus in detail on modern lightweight equipment (see 'Equipment'). We also believe that it is crucial to match your itinerary to your experience, fitness and ability. Accordingly, we have included here an extraordinary level of detail on itinerary planning: our unique itinerary planner has 14 different itineraries to choose from. For each itinerary, we have completed for you all the difficult calculations of time, distance and altitude gain/loss. This makes it easy for you to design a manageable itinerary that suits your specific needs. Once on the trail, you will be able to relax and fully enjoy one of the world's great treks.

Basic facts about Iceland

▶ Iceland is Europe's second largest island (after Great Britain): it is approximately 500km wide and 300km tall, with a surface area of 103,000 km^2

▶ The mainland is only 40km from the Arctic Circle

▶ Capital: Reykjavík

▶ Population: approximately 370,000. Two-thirds of the population live near Reykjavík

▶ Iceland has 11,000 km^2 of lava fields and 12,000 km^2 of glaciers

▶ Highest point: Hvannadalshnúkur (2119m)

▶ Iceland has the world's youngest island: Surtsey rose from the sea during volcanic activity in the 1960s

How hard are the LT and FT?

On paper at least, the LT does not appear to be terribly difficult: for a multi-day trek, the distance and altitude gain/loss are relatively modest. However, these bare statistics do not tell the full story and the LT can be harder than you might think. Accordingly, it should not be undertaken lightly and it is important to be sure that you understand what you are getting into before you start.

The LT's main route is 56km long and, with one exception, the distance between overnight stops is more than 11km. Accordingly, you will need to walk a significant distance each day. It crosses remote landscapes of volcanic mountains, hills and valleys: you will need to climb and descend significantly, on a daily basis, to negotiate the undulating terrain. Sometimes, the climbs and descents are steep and challenging. As the days go by, such exertions take their toll on your body, both physically and mentally.

The demand on your body is intensified by the need to carry more in your pack than on many other European treks: in addition to clothes and other necessities, you will have to carry a lot of food because there are few places on the LT to buy supplies. Furthermore, everyone (including those who sleep in the huts) will need to carry a sleeping bag. And because the huts are small and book up quickly, most trekkers carry their own camping equipment too, further increasing pack weight. It is fair to say that many trekkers set off carrying some equipment which is unnecessary or simply too heavy: this often results in injury and/or exhaustion, leading to abandonment. Of the difficulties discussed here, this is the only one that you have any control over. You should therefore give equipment choice careful consideration: it will be crucial to your enjoyment of the trek and the likelihood of success.

Another factor to consider is Iceland's notoriously poor and changeable weather. Those who experience fine weather throughout the trek can consider themselves to be very lucky indeed. Even in summer, it can be very wet and windy, making the trek more challenging.

For the most part, the LT uses clear paths and tracks which are well-marked and simple to follow. However, occasionally paths are less obvious and are more difficult to navigate. Sometimes paths are steep, rocky and challenging underfoot. Occasionally, you might have to climb up or down a few boulders but fortunately, you will not require any technical scrambling or climbing skills. However, there are five rivers to cross and a few of these crossings are pretty difficult if the water is high: for further information, see p39.

Although the LT is generally easier than many Alpine treks (such as the Tour du Mont Blanc), which are longer and have more climbing/descending, a reasonable level of fitness is still required: the fitter you are at the start of the trek, the better your chances of success and the more you will enjoy it. It is sensible to train in advance: there is no substitute for training hikes, carrying a pack. Although not absolutely necessary, previous experience of backpacking and camping will help.

The FT is more difficult than the LT. It involves a long and relentless climb which is far more challenging than any on the LT. There are steep and exposed sections, with sheer drops, where a fall could be serious: occasionally, ropes/chains are fixed to the rocks for safety. Accordingly, the FT is not suitable for those with a fear of heights. The huts near the Fimmvörðuháls pass are more basic than those on the LT and little drinking water is available there: N-S trekkers will have to carry water up from the bottom of the climb if they wish to stay overnight.

Most people walk the LT in 3 or 4 days. However, fit and experienced hikers can finish it in 2 days and endurance runners often do it even faster. Others prefer to walk more slowly, allowing 5 days to soak up all of the delights on offer: with spare time, you could walk a few of the excellent side routes which we also describe here. Most people aim to complete the FT in one day but this is a long and challenging undertaking which leaves little time to explore the eruption sites near the Fimmvörðuháls pass or to enjoy the waterfalls along the Skógá River: 2 days provides the time to enjoy the FT fully but you would have to stay at one of the basic huts and carry more drinking water. It would be normal to hike both the LT and the FT in a total of 4 to 6 days.

Direction and start/finish points

The LT runs between Landmannalaugar in the N and Þórsmörk in the S. The FT runs between the end of the LT in Þórsmörk and Skógar (further S). Daily buses serve all three of these places as well as Húsadalur (Stage v4b/v4c; OR) and Básar (Stage 5a/5b). As you can hike the trails in either direction, this book caters for both N-S and S-N trekkers: full route descriptions and plenty of different itineraries are provided for each approach. The numbered waypoints on the maps make the route easy to follow in either direction.

Traditionally, people walk N-S and there are some compelling reasons for this approach:

▶ Landmannalaugar (the N trail-head) sits at 585m above sea level whereas Þórsmörk and Skógar (the two S trail-heads) are located at lower elevations (225m and 25m respectively): this means that it is easier to hike N-S because N-S trekkers have less climbing to endure than those heading S-N.

▶ The FT is harder than the LT and it is therefore preferable to tackle it last. N-S trekkers should be well warmed up by the time they undertake the long climb to the Fimmvörðuháls pass. However, S-N trekkers will begin the longest climb immediately after departure from Skógar (on the first day): that said, the climb to the Fimmvörðuháls pass is easier from the S because the gradient is usually less steep.

▶ In high season, the huts on the LT cannot be booked in a S-N direction. Accordingly, those who are not camping have no choice but to head N-S in peak season. If you are intending to camp then you can still travel in either direction in peak season.

▶ In our opinion, there are a few parts of the trek that are better viewed heading S. For example, reaching the S rim of the Torfajökull Caldera is one of the LT's most memorable moments: the first glimpse of the view S over Álftavatn is exquisite and travelling S-N removes the element of surprise. Furthermore, hiking N-S allows you to spend more time gazing at the spectacular ice-capped Eyjafjallajökull volcano and the huge Mýrdalsjökull Glacier (because for the most part you will be walking towards them).

▶ The waterfalls of Stage 6b make for a euphoric ending to an incredible trek.

▶ The restaurant at Skógar is perfect for a post-trek celebration.

▶ Broadly speaking, the landscape becomes greener and less barren the further S you get. Heading S, the climate also becomes milder as you lose altitude and approach the coast. If you head S-N, the increasing starkness and dropping temperatures can be more overwhelming.

▶ The river crossings get harder as you head S. This means that N-S trekkers start with the easier ones and work up to the Þröngá River which is the most challenging. S-N trekkers, on the other hand, will be plunged in at the deep end (pun intended!) by having to tackle the most difficult crossing first.

▶ As most walkers travel N-S, that is probably the more sociable approach: you are more likely to bump into the same people each day, making it easier to develop trail friendships.

However, there are also a few good reasons for hiking S-N:

▶ The fumaroles and rainbow mountains of Section 1 are a scenic highlight of the LT and are a fabulous climax to the trek.

▶ At the end of your journey, it is wonderful to soak aching muscles in the hot springs at Landmannalaugar.

▶ The climb to the Fimmvörðuháls pass is easier from the S because the gradient is usually less steep.

The bridge over the Kaldaklofskvísl River (Stage 3b)

Hiking shorter sections of the LT/FT

Walking the LT and FT in one go is a wonderful experience but there are other ways to enjoy these incredible trails. If you do not wish to spend nights on the trail, you could, for example, hike the entire FT as a day-hike. It is also possible to walk some sections of the LT as day-walks. During the hiking season, daily buses serve Landmannalaugar (Stage 1), Langidalur Hut at Þórsmörk (Stage 4b/5a), Húsadalur (Stage v4b/v4c; OR), Básar (Stage 5a/5b) and Skógar (Stage 6b): there are day-walks along the LT/FT from each of these places.

If you only wish to walk some of the highlights of the region, then we would suggest some or all of the following options:

▶ **The Rainbow Mountains of Section 1 (5-5.5hr):** see map on p73. Hike from Landmannalaugar to **(4)** along the route of Stage 1. Then retrace your steps to **(2)**: from there, use Stage v1a or v1b to return to Landmannalaugar.

▶ **Tindfjöll Circuit (3.75hr):** see p97 for this circular day-walk from Þórsmörk.

▶ **The Knife Edge Ridge of Section 5 (5.5hr):** see map on p96. Hike from Básar to **(3)**. Then retrace your steps to Básar.

▶ **The Waterfalls of Section 6 (5.5hr):** see map on p114. Hike from Skógar to **(1)**. Then retrace your steps to Skógar.

Guided tours, self-guided tours or independent walking?

A frequently asked question is whether to walk independently or with an organised group. The answer is a personal one and depends upon your own particular circumstances and requirements. For many, the decision to organise the trek themselves, and to walk independently, can be almost life-changing, opening the door for other challenges in the future. There is much satisfaction to be gained from planning and navigating a trek yourself and the sense of achievement on completion is to be savoured.

However, the independent trekker usually carries a full pack and is responsible for all daily decisions such as pacing, which way to go at junctions, when to stock up with food and water, and choice of route in bad weather. For some, this may be too great a burden on top of the physical effort required simply to walk the route. For those walkers, a guided group is a great solution: the tour company typically organises food, accommodation and transfer of luggage each night. And the guide makes all the decisions, enabling the walker to concentrate on the walking. There are some tour companies which operate guided trips on the LT: they do not always provide food on the trail so check before booking.

There are also some businesses offering self-guided tours on the LT and these are a sensible middle-ground. The tour company books all the accommodation and provides advice and information on walking the route. However, you will walk the trail without a guide. They do not always provide food on the trail so check before booking. Often, they can transfer your baggage to your accommodation each night so you only need to carry a small day-pack on the trail. Even confident trekkers (who would be perfectly capable of walking independently) may benefit from booking a self-guided trip simply to avail of the accommodation booking service. By booking a self-guided tour, much of the hassle of planning the trek is alleviated, albeit at a price.

When to go

Iceland's location close to the Arctic Circle means that the weather window for hiking the LT/FT is quite short: the trekking season starts towards the end of June and ends around the middle of September. However, even in this period, high winds, heavy rain, and low cloud (which reduces visibility), are common: occasionally, it can even snow on the trail. You might get lucky and hike in fine weather but you should prepare for the worst. Throughout the trekking season, there is plenty of daylight. The relative merits of each season are discussed in detail below but, taking all the factors into consideration, we prefer to hike the LT/FT in the last 2 weeks of August.

Late June: the LT usually opens for the season towards the end of June but the actual date changes from year to year. This is because access to the trail is not possible until the Icelandic Road Authority opens the roads to Landmannalaugar and this does not happen until the snow has been cleared from the road (see **www.road.is**). This can be a beautiful time of year for walking but there will still be plenty of snow lying on the trail: fortunately, the trail is marked with tall posts but you will have to follow them carefully because they can be hard to spot against the snow. The trail will become quickly tracked by others ahead of you but always be wary of following someone else's footprints: there is a good chance that they are on the correct path but it is obviously possible that they may have strayed from the trail. Also, remember that any fresh snow will obscure other's footprints. The rivers will be running high because of snow-melt and therefore the river crossings are most difficult at this time of year. The FT can be a challenge in June and fresh snow is a possibility. The days are longest in this period and, in fact, because Iceland is close to the Arctic Circle, there is almost no darkness at all. Although the LT/FT are not famous for flowers, some wild-flowers do begin to show themselves as snow clears. The number of hikers gradually increases throughout the month.

July: this is the peak month for trekking the LT/FT. The trails are at their busiest and hut accommodation is hard to find. Book well in advance unless you are camping. Early in the month, you may still find plenty of snow in the Torfajökull Caldera (Sections 1 and 2): see above. As the month progresses, there will be less snow on the trail and river crossings will become less difficult.

August: the first half of August is normally as busy as July. Hut accommodation is hard to find: book well in advance for this period unless you are camping. However, from the middle of August, the number of trekkers starts to decrease. As the month progresses further, the days become gradually shorter and temperatures gradually drop: there is still plenty of daylight for hiking though. Although huts are still busy, it becomes easier to find a bed: sometimes, availability opens up at the last minute. There should only be a little snow left on the trail and river crossings will be easier.

September: the LT usually closes for the season towards the middle of September but the actual date changes from year to year. This is because access to the trail is not possible after the Icelandic Road Authority closes the roads to Landmannalaugar and that is weather-dependent (see **www.road.is**). As the month progresses, the days get even shorter and temperatures drop further: there is still plenty of daylight for hiking though and the weather can still be favourable. Morning and evening temperatures can be pretty low so carry a winter sleeping bag. Fresh snow becomes more likely as the month progresses. The weather on high parts of the FT can be very bad in September.

Month	Pros	Cons
Late June	Fewer trekkers **Hut beds easier to find** Longest days	Most snow on trail **River crossings most difficult**
July	Best chance of fine weather **Long days**	Visitor numbers highest **Hut beds hard to find** Plenty of snow early in month **River crossings difficult early in month**
1st half of August	Best chance of fine weather **Long days**	Visitor numbers highest **Hut beds hard to find**
2nd half of August	Good chance of fine weather **Still plenty of daylight** Fewer trekkers as month progresses **Hut beds become easier to find** Trail almost clear of snow **River crossings easier**	Temperatures dropping
September	Sufficient daylight **Fewer trekkers** Hut beds easier to find **Trail usually clear of snow** River crossings usually easier	Cold mornings/evenings **Fresh snow becoming more likely** Huts close around the middle of the month **Weather on the FT can be bad**

Iceland's flag flying in the Hvanngil Valley (Stage 3a)

Using this book

This book is designed to be used by walkers of differing abilities. Many guidebooks for long-distance treks rigidly divide the route into a fixed number of long day-stages, leaving it up to the hiker to break down those stages to design daily routes which suit his/her abilities. This book, however, has been laid out differently to give the trekker flexibility: it divides the LT/FT route into 10 shorter stages which you can combine to design daily routes that meet your own specific needs.

Generally, each stage covers the distance between one accommodation option and the subsequent one: Stages 4a, 4b, 5b and 6a are exceptions as they have accommodation at one end and a significant junction at the other. All accommodation options on the route are the start/finish point of a stage. You can choose how many of these stages you wish to walk each day. Each stage has its own walk description, route map and elevation profile.

The labelling of the stages uses a combination of numbers and letters. It is a simple system but requires a little bit of explanation. Firstly, we have divided the LT/FT route into 6 'Sections' (numbered from 1 to 6 from N-S): each Section represents one day of our standard 6-day schedule. Within some Sections, the route has been further broken down into two stages: these stages are labelled with a number between 1 and 6, representing the relevant Section that the stage is part of. These stages are also labelled with a letter. So, for example, the first stage in Section 3 is 'Stage 3a' and the second stage is 'Stage 3b'. Take a look at the detailed Itinerary Planner below and all should become clear.

The Itinerary Planner includes a range of tables outlining 14 suggested itineraries of 2, 3, 4, 5, 6 and 7 days. We include itineraries for both N-S and S-N trekkers. In each table, the maths have been done for you so there is no need for you to waste time (and mental strength) working out daily distances, timings and altitude gain/loss.

Of course, the suggested itineraries are only suggestions. You can shorten or lengthen your day to suit yourself: just decide how many stages you want to walk that day. It is up to you. As there is accommodation/camping at the end of most stages, it is easy to design your own bespoke itinerary and adjust it on the ground as you go.

For example, day 3 of the standard 6-day itinerary involves walking Stages 3a and 3b. However, you could decide to extend your day by walking Stages 3a, 3b and 4a, all on the same day. Or you might be tired and decide to shorten your day by walking only Stage 3a. With some other guidebooks, you would have to work out how to split stages yourself, involving some complicated maths to plan distances and times going forward. This guide, however, does all the hard mental work for you.

In this book:

Timings indicate the approximate time required by a reasonably fit walker to complete a stage. They include the time taken to negotiate river crossings on the route. However, they do not include stoppage time. Do not get frustrated if your own times do not match ours: everyone walks at different speeds. As you progress through the trek, you will soon learn how your own times compare with those given here and you will adjust your plans accordingly.

Walking distances are given in both miles and kilometres (km). One mile equates to approximately 1.6km.

Place names in brackets in the route descriptions indicate the direction to be followed on signposts. For example, "('Álftavatn')" would mean that you follow a sign for Álftavatn.

Ascent/descent numbers are the aggregate of all the altitude gain or loss (measured in feet and metres) on the uphill or downhill sections of a stage. As a rule of thumb, a fit walker climbs 1000 to 1300 feet (300 to 400m) in an hour. The statistics tables in the route descriptions are based on N-S itineraries: S-N trekkers should simply swap the ascent and descent figures.

Elevation profiles are provided for each Section, indicating where the climbs and descents fall on the route. The profiles are based on N-S itineraries: S-N walkers should simply read them in reverse.

Real maps are provided. These are extracts from 1:40,000 scale maps produced by Knife Edge Outdoor Guidebooks. We believe that these are the best maps available for the LT/FT. On the maps, we have marked the route of the trek, the start/finish points of stages, significant waypoints and the accommodation along the LT/FT. On each map, N is at the top of the page. As well as printing these maps in this book, we have also published a sheet map for the LT/FT which is extremely helpful for planning and navigation: *'The Laugavegur Trail & the Fimmvörðuháls Trail'* (ISBN: 9781912933501).

The following abbreviations are used:

BCE	Before the Common Era (a secular alternative to 'BC')
CE	The Common Era (a secular alternative to 'AD')
FÍ	Ferðafélag Íslands, the Iceland Touring Association
FT	Fimmvörðuháls Trail
ISK	Icelandic Krona (Iceland's currency)
LT	Laugavegur Trail
OR	Off-route
RE	Reykjavík Excursions
WW2	World War 2
TL	Turn left
TR	Turn right
SH	Straight ahead
N, S, E and W, etc.	North, South, East and West, etc.
N-S	North to South
S-N	South to North

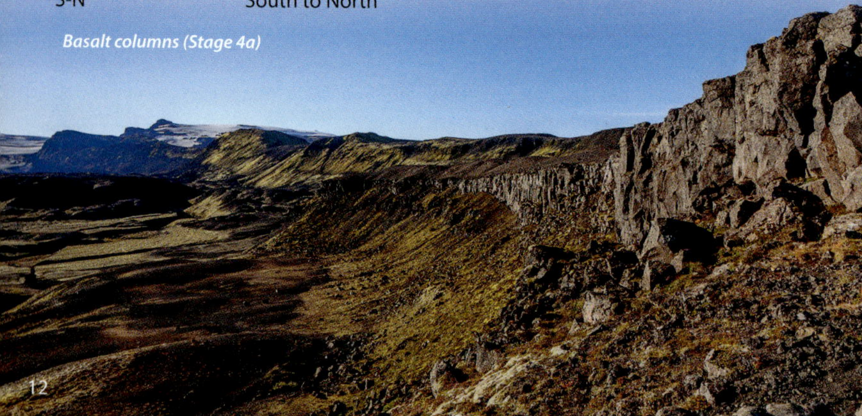
Basalt columns (Stage 4a)

Itinerary Planner: North to South

Stage	Start	Time (hr)	Distance km	Distance miles	Ascent m	Ascent ft	Descent m	Descent ft
1	Landmannalaugar	4:30	11.7	7.3	680	2231	233	764
2	Hrafntinnusker	4:30	12.1	7.5	240	787	722	2369
3a	Álftavatn	1:30	4.2	2.6	154	505	148	486
3b	Hvanngil	4:15	12.2	7.6	196	643	287	942
4a	Emstrur/Botnar	5:45	14.7	9.1	380	1247	580	1903
4b	Húsadalur north exit	0:30	1.5	0.9	60	197	100	328
5a	Þórsmörk (Langidalur)	0:30	2.2	1.4	0	0	0	0
5b	Básar	5:15	10.7	6.7	977	3206	192	630
6a	Fimmvörðuháls exit	0:30	1.4	0.9	35	115	140	459
6b	Baldvinsskáli	4:00	13.7	8.5	122	400	1002	3288
Finish	Skógar							

Itinerary Planner: South to North

Stage	Start	Time (hr)	Distance km	Distance miles	Ascent m	Ascent ft	Descent m	Descent ft
6b	Skógar	5:30	13.7	8.5	1002	3288	122	400
6a	Baldvinsskáli	0:45	1.4	0.9	140	459	35	115
5b	Fimmvörðuháls exit	4:00	10.7	6.7	192	630	977	3206
5a	Básar	0:30	2.2	1.4	0	0	0	0
4b	Þórsmörk (Langidalur)	0:30	1.5	0.9	100	328	60	197
4a	Húsadalur north exit	6:15	14.7	9.1	580	1903	380	1247
3b	Emstrur/Botnar	4:30	12.2	7.6	287	942	196	643
3a	Hvanngil	1:30	4.2	2.6	148	486	154	505
2	Álftavatn	5:30	12.1	7.5	722	2369	240	787
1	Hrafntinnusker	4:00	11.7	7.3	233	764	680	2231
Finish	Landmannalaugar							

The River Bratthálskvísl (Stage 3a)

Suggested Itineraries: North to South

For completeness, all our itineraries incorporate both the LT (Sections 1 to 4) and the FT (Sections 5 and 6). However, because the FT is harder than the LT, many hikers choose to hike only the LT. If you do not wish to walk the FT, simply remove sections 5 and 6 from the relevant itinerary.

7 Days (5 days LT, 2 days FT): our most leisurely itinerary which is great for those with plenty of time. Although Day 3 is very short, you could spend some time exploring the beautiful landscape around Hvanngil Hut. The first stage is tough with plenty of climbing but there is no way around that.

Day	Stages	Time (hr)	Distance		Ascent		Descent	
			km	miles	m	ft	m	ft
1	1	4:30	11.7	7.3	680	2231	233	764
2	2	4:30	12.1	7.5	240	787	722	2369
3	3a	1:30	4.2	2.6	154	505	148	486
4	3b	4:15	12.2	7.6	196	643	287	942
5	4a, 4b	6:15	16.2	10.1	440	1444	680	2231
6	5a, 5b	5:45	12.9	8.0	977	3206	192	630
7	6a, 6b	4:30	15.1	9.4	157	515	1142	3747

6 Days Option A (4 days LT, 2 days FT): our standard schedule which is popular with many walkers because it is well-balanced, dividing the route into manageable stages. The first stage is tough with plenty of climbing but there is no way around that. Day 2 allows a bit of respite before the longer stages begin.

Day	Stages	Time (hr)	Distance		Ascent		Descent	
			km	miles	m	ft	m	ft
1	1	4:30	11.7	7.3	680	2231	233	764
2	2	4:30	12.1	7.5	240	787	722	2369
3	3a, 3b	5:45	16.4	10.2	350	1148	435	1427
4	4a, 4b	6:15	16.2	10.1	440	1444	680	2231
5	5a, 5b	5:45	12.9	8.0	977	3206	192	630
6	6a, 6b	4:30	15.1	9.4	157	515	1142	3747

6 Days Option B (4 days LT, 2 days FT): identical to 6 Days Option A except that you travel further on day 2, spending the night at Hvanngil which can be more peaceful than Álftavatn. This makes day 3 shorter and easier.

Day	Stages	Time (hr)	Distance		Ascent		Descent	
			km	miles	m	ft	m	ft
1	1	4:30	11.7	7.3	680	2231	233	764
2	2, 3a	6:00	16.3	10.1	394	1293	870	2854
3	3b	4:15	12.2	7.6	196	643	287	942
4	4a, 4b	6:15	16.2	10.1	440	1444	680	2231
5	5a, 5b	5:45	12.9	8.0	977	3206	192	630
6	6a, 6b	4:30	15.1	9.4	157	515	1142	3747

5 Days (4 days LT, 1 day FT):
similar to 6 Days Option A except that you walk most of the FT in one day. Furthermore, on day 4 you will stay at Básar (rather than Langidalur) so that you start the following day at the base of the climb. Although day 5 is extremely long, this is a popular itinerary because it avoids the need to spend a night at the basic huts on the Fimmvörðuháls pass: often no drinking water is available there and those staying overnight have to carry it up from Básar, making for a heavy load on the hardest climb of the entire trek.

Day	Stages	Time (hr)	Distance		Ascent		Descent	
			km	miles	m	ft	m	ft
1	1	4:30	11.7	7.3	680	2231	233	764
2	2	4:30	12.1	7.5	240	787	722	2369
3	3a, 3b	5:45	16.4	10.2	350	1148	435	1427
4	4a, 4b, 5a	6:45	18.4	11.4	440	1444	680	2231
5	5b, 6a, 6b	9:45	25.8	16.0	1134	3721	1334	4377

4 Days (3 days LT and 1 day FT):
a tough itinerary which will suit fit and experienced hikers who arrive at the start in good shape. The first stage is very tough. Days 2 and 3 are comparatively easier and provide some respite before the challenging final day.

Day	Stages	Time (hr)	Distance		Ascent		Descent	
			km	miles	m	ft	m	ft
1	1, 2	9:00	23.8	14.8	920	3019	955	3133
2	3a, 3b	5:45	16.4	10.2	350	1148	435	1427
3	4a, 4b, 5a	6:45	18.4	11.4	440	1444	680	2231
4	5b, 6a, 6b	9:45	25.8	16.0	1134	3721	1334	4377

3 Days (2 days LT and 1 day FT):
an extremely challenging itinerary for very fit and experienced hikers only. Every day is very tough.

Day	Stages	Time (hr)	Distance		Ascent		Descent	
			km	miles	m	ft	m	ft
1	1, 2, 3a	10:30	28.0	17.4	1074	3524	1103	3619
2	3b, 4a, 4b	10:30	28.4	17.7	636	2087	967	3173
3	5a, 5b, 6a, 6b	10:15	28.0	17.4	1134	3721	1334	4377

2 Days:
a brutal itinerary for experienced trail-runners.

Day	Stages	Time (hr)	Distance		Ascent		Descent	
			km	miles	m	ft	m	ft
1	1, 2, 3a, 3b	14:45	40.2	25.0	1270	4167	1390	4561
2	4a, 4b, 5a, 5b, 6a, 6b	16:30	44.2	27.5	1574	5164	2014	6608

Suggested Itineraries: South to North

For completeness, all our itineraries incorporate both the LT (Sections 1 to 4) and the FT (Sections 5 and 6). However, because the FT is harder than the LT, many hikers choose to hike only the LT. If you do not wish to walk the FT, simply remove sections 5 and 6 from the relevant itinerary.

For those walking both the FT and the LT, a S-N approach is a tougher proposition because the journey begins with the hardest climb of the entire trek: from Skógar, you will start the 1000m climb to Fimmvörðuháls without any warm up at all.

7 Days (2 days FT, 5 days LT): our most leisurely itinerary which is great for those with plenty of time. Although day 5 is very short, you could spend some time exploring the beautiful landscape around Hvanngil Hut. The first stage is very tough with plenty of climbing. Then, day 2 involves a long descent to Þórsmörk (Langidalur).

Day	Stages	Time (hr)	Distance		Ascent		Descent	
			km	miles	m	ft	m	ft
1	6b, 6a	6:15	15.1	9.4	1142	3747	157	515
2	5b, 5a	4:30	12.9	8.0	192	630	977	3206
3	4b, 4a	6:45	16.2	10.1	680	2231	440	1444
4	3b	4:30	12.2	7.6	287	942	196	643
5	3a	1:30	4.2	2.7	148	486	154	505
6	2	5:30	12.1	7.5	722	2369	240	787
7	1	4:00	11.7	7.3	233	764	680	2231

6 Days Option A (2 days FT, 4 days LT): our standard schedule is well-balanced, dividing the route into manageable stages. The first day is very tough with plenty of climbing. Then, day 2 involves a long, knee-jerking descent.

Day	Stages	Time (hr)	Distance		Ascent		Descent	
			km	miles	m	ft	m	ft
1	6b, 6a	6:15	15.1	9.4	1142	3747	157	515
2	5b, 5a	4:30	12.9	8.0	192	630	977	3206
3	4b, 4a	6:45	16.2	10.1	680	2231	440	1444
4	3b, 3a	6:00	16.4	10.3	435	1427	350	1148
5	2	5:30	12.1	7.5	722	2369	240	787
6	1	4:00	11.7	7.3	233	764	680	2231

6 Days Option B (2 days FT, 4 days LT): identical to 6 Days Option A except that you travel further on day 5, after spending the night at Hvanngil. Although there is a lot of climbing on day 5, day 4 is shorter and easier.

Day	Stages	Time (hr)	Distance		Ascent		Descent	
			km	miles	m	ft	m	ft
1	6b, 6a	6:15	15.1	9.4	1142	3747	157	515
2	5b, 5a	4:30	12.9	8.0	192	630	977	3206
3	4b, 4a	6:45	16.2	10.1	680	2231	440	1444
4	3b	4:30	12.2	7.6	287	942	196	643
5	3a, 2	7:00	16.3	10.3	870	2854	394	1293
6	1	4:00	11.7	7.3	233	764	680	2231

5 Days (1 day FT, 4 days LT): similar to 6 Days Option A except that you trek most of the FT in one day. You will need to be in good shape at the start of the trek. Although day 1 is extremely long, this is a popular itinerary because it avoids the need to spend a night at the basic huts on the Fimmvörðuháls pass. Instead, you will stay at Básar.

Day	Stages	Time (hr)	Distance		Ascent		Descent	
			km	miles	m	ft	m	ft
1	6b, 6a, 5b	10:15	25.8	16.0	1334	4377	1134	3721
2	5a, 4b, 4a	7:15	18.4	11.4	680	2231	440	1444
3	3b, 3a	6:00	16.4	10.3	435	1427	350	1148
4	2	5:30	12.1	7.5	722	2369	240	787
5	1	4:00	11.7	7.3	233	764	680	2231

4 Days (1 day FT, 3 days LT): a tough itinerary which will suit fit and experienced hikers who arrive at the start in good shape. The first stage is extremely tough. Days 2 and 3 are comparatively easier and provide some respite before the challenging final day.

Day	Stages	Time (hr)	Distance		Ascent		Descent	
			km	miles	m	ft	m	ft
1	6b, 6a, 5b	10:15	25.8	16.0	1334	4377	1134	3721
2	5a, 4b, 4a	7:15	18.4	11.4	680	2231	440	1444
3	3b, 3a	6:00	16.4	10.3	435	1427	350	1148
4	2, 1	9:30	23.8	14.8	955	3133	920	3019

3 Days (1 day FT, 2 days LT): an extremely challenging itinerary for very fit and experienced hikers only. Every day is very tough.

Day	Stages	Time (hr)	Distance		Ascent		Descent	
			km	miles	m	ft	m	ft
1	6b, 6a, 5b	10:15	25.8	16.0	1334	4377	1134	3721
2	5a, 4b, 4a, 3b	11:45	30.6	19.0	967	3173	636	2087
3	3a, 2, 1	11:00	28.0	17.5	1103	3619	1074	3524

2 Days: a brutal itinerary for experienced trail-runners.

Day	Stages	Time (hr)	Distance		Ascent		Descent	
			km	miles	m	ft	m	ft
1	6b, 6a, 5b, 5a, 4b, 4a	17:30	44.2	27.5	2014	6608	1574	5164
2	3b, 3a, 2, 1	15:30	40.2	25.1	1390	4561	1270	4167

Accommodation

*Langidalur Hut
(Stage 4b/5a)*

Reykjavík accommodation

Reykjavík has no shortage of accommodation: there are hotels, guesthouses, hostels and a campsite. Although some places are less expensive than others, none of them are cheap. The generic travel booking sites (such as expedia.com and booking.com) are a good place to start your research because they feature a wide variety of Reykjavík's hotels, guesthouses and hostels.

Hotels: these range from basic hotels to more luxury properties. In the trekking season, it is occasionally possible to get a basic room for less than €100 but usually you will pay more than that. At the upper end of the scale, you could spend many hundreds of euros. Generally, the closer to the tourist centre, the more expensive the hotels become. Most properties provide breakfast and evening meals: alternatively, Reykjavík has no shortage of cafés and restaurants. Most hotels have their own websites.

Guesthouses: these offer bed & breakfast style accommodation. Traditionally, they were private homes which had been converted to offer private rooms to visitors. Nowadays, however, you find many bigger and more professionally run properties. Often, they have buildings which were added specifically for guests. Most of the rooms have ensuite bathroom facilities but occasionally, you might have to share a bathroom. They are usually clean and comfortable. In Reykjavík, guesthouses often cost the same as a lower budget hotel.

Hostels: these offer beds in dormitories and basic private rooms. Sometimes rooms have ensuite bathrooms but often you will share one. There are usually self-catering kitchen facilities and communal areas. Continental breakfast is sometimes available. Bedding is usually supplied. Hostels are becoming more upmarket and prices rise along with the quality of the offering. Beds start at around €45 per person. Groups of two or more may find guesthouses or hotels to be better value. Reykjavík HI Hostel, E of the city centre, is a good choice because both RE/Trex buses stop there on their way to/from Landmannalaugar/Þórsmörk/Skógar: see **www.hostel.is**.

Campsite: for those on a tighter budget, Reykjavík's campsite is an excellent option (**www.reykjavíkcampsite.is**). It costs around 3,200 ISK per person per night and is located E of the city centre, beside Reykjavík HI Hostel (see above): RE/Trex buses stop there on their way to/from Landmannalaugar/Þórsmörk/Skógar and most airport buses stop too. The campsite has self-catering kitchen facilities, WiFi and luggage storage. Within walking distance, there are ATMs, grocery stores and gas stations. Often trekkers leave behind unwanted food/gas in the kitchen for others to take. Nearby, there are also restaurants, cafés and a swimming pool (with hot tubs).

Accommodation along the trail

For accommodation along the LT/FT, you have two main options: dormitory beds at mountain huts or camping. Additionally, the privately owned Volcano Huts at Húsadalur has slightly more upmarket accommodation: it is 1.7km OR from the Langidalur Hut at Þórsmörk. Furthermore, at Skógar (the S trail-head), there is a hotel as well as a campsite.

All accommodation is numbered and marked on the maps in this book. Detailed accommodation listings are provided on pages 22 and 23. All contact details were correct at the date of press but this information frequently changes (particularly, in the aftermath of Covid-19 which has had a significant and lasting impact on the travel industry). Please let us know about any changes you notice.

Huts: these basic buildings have spectacular settings. You will sleep in mixed-sex dormitories: sometimes there are beds (with mattresses) but in other places, you will sleep on mattresses on the floor. Although mattresses are provided, you will need to bring your own sleeping bag. There are usually gas fires inside to warm the living quarters but the dormitories can be cold. Each hut has a kitchen (with gas stoves/pots/utensils/washing-up liquid) which you can use if you are staying in the hut. All the huts on the LT have toilets and running water for drinking/washing: they all have showers too

(additional fee: 500 ISK) except Hrafntinnusker. On the FT, only Básar has showers and drinking/washing water. If you wish to use toilet facilities at a hut that you are not staying at, then you may be asked to pay a facility fee (500 ISK): this is not always enforced.

All LT huts accept credit cards, however, on the FT, only Básar accepts them. The huts do not provide food so you must bring your own (see p25). Although the huts on the LT sell basic provisions, stocks can vary and there is no guarantee that you will find what you need: gas canisters, freeze-dried backpacking meals, candy, beer and sodas are usually available. There are no charging facilities for electronic devices but you can usually buy battery charging packs. On the FT, do not expect to find any supplies. Some huts do not have garbage facilities and you should pack out all your own rubbish.

The huts are normally clean, well run and open throughout the walking season (roughly mid-June to mid-September). Along the LT, all six huts are operated by Ferðafélag Íslands, the Iceland Touring Association (FÍ). On the FT, only Baldvinsskáli is operated by FÍ: Básar and Fimmvörðuháls/Fimmvörðuskáli are operated by Útivist (see Accommodation Listings).

For the 2023 season, FÍ's huts on the LT cost 11,000 ISK per person per night. The huts on the FT are a little cheaper because the facilities are more basic. To book the FÍ huts, you must first enquire about availability by filling in the online form at **www.fi.is**: you do not need to pay at this stage. FÍ will respond a few days later to confirm whether or not there is availability. If your dates are available, then they will send you a secure payment link: you click on it and make payment by credit card. You should pay as quickly as possible to ensure that you do not lose the dates. After you have paid, FÍ will send you a booking confirmation.

These days, you generally need to book huts well in advance, especially in July and the first half of August. In June, the second half of August and September, if you are lucky, you may find availability at late notice. Realistically, you should book huts as soon as booking opens: this normally happens around the end of the previous season. Because FÍ has a favourable cancellation policy, many people snap up beds even if they are not sure that they will ultimately use them: you get 85% back if you cancel 30 days or more before arrival. This means that the beds book up very quickly indeed: at the time of writing (December 2022), all LT hut beds for 2023 were already sold out. However, do not necessarily give up if you cannot find availability: beds can free up when people cancel later on so check again closer to the time. Furthermore, because there is no refund for cancellations less than seven days before arrival, many people who have to cancel their trip at the last minute simply do not turn up: usually, these beds are available, on the day, on a first come, first served basis. However, there is no guarantee of finding an available bed on arrival at the hut so you will need to carry a tent anyway. Also bear in mind that if the weather is bad, every camper will have similar thoughts and the beds will go to the first people who ask.

Camping: at each hut, there is a camp-ground. You do not need to book in advance to pitch your tent so camping provides much more flexibility: you can change your itinerary while on the trail. On arrival at the hut, you should pay your fee at the hut office: the warden will give you a tag to affix to your tent to prove that you have paid. After paying, you may pitch your tent. For the 2023 season, the camping fee was 2,500 ISK per person per night. All LT huts accept credit cards, however, on the FT, only Básar accepts them.

Campers may use the huts' toilets and washing facilities: showers (if any) cost 500 ISK extra. Campers are not permitted to enter the huts or use the kitchen facilities: bring your own stove, pot, utensils and gas. Landmannalaugar, Emstrur/Botnar and Langidalur have marquee-style tents in which campers may eat. At some huts, there are no garbage facilities so be prepared to pack out all your own rubbish.

In response to the increase in visitors to Iceland, the laws and rules on wild camping have changed in recent years. According to the website of Umhverfis Stofnun (Iceland's Environment Agency), Article 22 of the Nature Conservation Act (which came into force in 2015) states that *'Traditional camping tents are allowed to be set up….. in the wilderness, whether on private land or public land'.* Furthermore, it adds that *'it is permitted to pitch traditional camping tents unless otherwise stated in special regulations that may apply to the area'.*

The website also states: *'It is allowed to camp for one night on uncultivated land. Landowners are required to indicate exceptions to that rule with signs. Out of consideration for the land and its owners, people should use marked camping areas if possible….. Groups must, without exception, consult with the rights holders of the land if they intend to pitch a tent outside the marked camping areas'.*

All of that seems to suggest that wild camping is legal unless: (1) the landowner expressly forbids it (with signs); (2) specific prohibitions have been implemented in the relevant area; or (3) you are in a group. As regards the LT/FT, we understand that specific regulations expressly prohibit wild camping within the Fjallabak Nature Reserve and around Skógafoss: this means that wild camping is definitely not permitted within the Torfajökull

Caldera (on Sections 1 and 2) or in the zone around the Skógafoss waterfall (Stage 6b). As regards the remainder of the LT/FT, we cannot find any special regulations that expressly prohibit wild camping so it may well be permitted. However, whether or not it is legal, it is generally frowned upon and we would not be in favour of it on the LT/FT: there are a lot of hikers and the landscape is fragile. For further information see, **www.ust.is**.

Dry-stone wind-break at Hrafntinnusker (Stage 1/2)

Hut etiquette

▶ On arrival, check in at the warden's office.

▶ Take off your boots and wet clothing at the front door and store them in the places provided at the entrance.

▶ Wash any pots, plates, cutlery straight away to allow others to use them.

▶ Do not make noise after 10pm as most walkers go to bed early.

▶ If you change your plans, cancel your reservation as soon as possible to allow someone else to take your place.

Booking tips

▶ The LT/FT becomes more popular each year. To ensure that you secure your accommodation of choice, book as early as you can. Many trekkers start booking in autumn (just after the current summer season has ended) for the following season.

▶ Start mid-week. Many trekkers start the trail at the weekend. Those who start mid-week are often 'out of sync' with the bulk of the trekkers and may therefore find accommodation more easily.

▶ Weekends are normally busier.

▶ Those who hike alone, or in pairs, will find it easiest to find beds. For larger groups, it is more difficult.

▶ If you cannot secure the accommodation that you need then contact a tour company. They sometimes pre-book accommodation in advance and may have spaces.

▶ Occasionally, the last-minute booker can get lucky: if you apply a few weeks before your trip, you may be lucky enough to bag some beds which have recently freed up as a result of cancellations.

Álftavatn Hut/Campsite (Stage 2/3a)

Accommodation Listings

 Hut Dormitory

 Private Room

 Camping

 Drinks

 Snacks

 Breakfast

 Lunch

 Evening Meals

 Grocery shop

 Basic supplies

 Toilets/ washbasins

 Showers

 Kitchen facilities

 Credit cards accepted

 WiFi

 **OR** Off-route

Volcanic peaks delicately frosted with moss (Stage 3b)

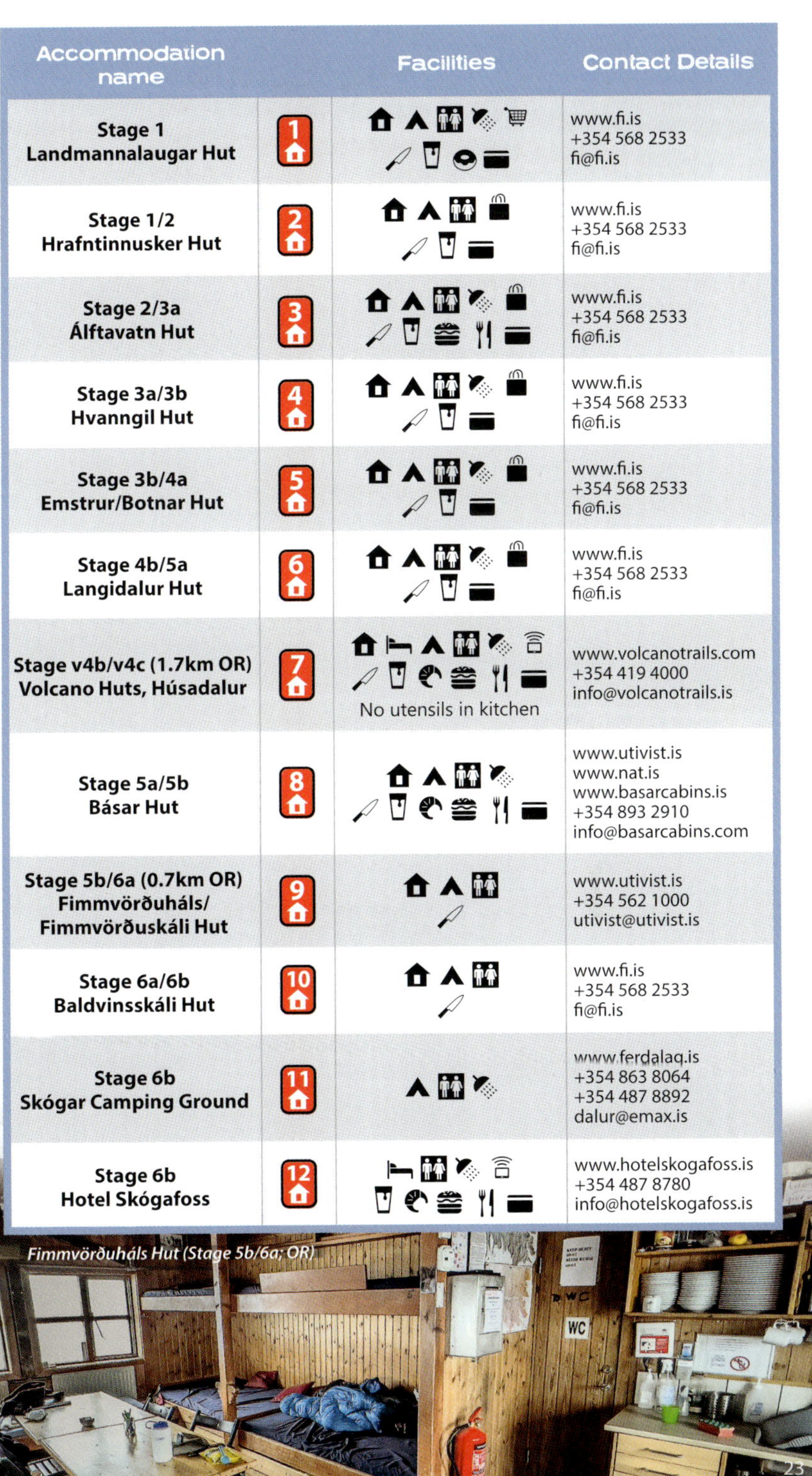

Accommodation name		Facilities	Contact Details
Stage 1 Landmannalaugar Hut	1		www.fi.is +354 568 2533 fi@fi.is
Stage 1/2 Hrafntinnusker Hut	2		www.fi.is +354 568 2533 fi@fi.is
Stage 2/3a Álftavatn Hut	3		www.fi.is +354 568 2533 fi@fi.is
Stage 3a/3b Hvanngil Hut	4		www.fi.is +354 568 2533 fi@fi.is
Stage 3b/4a Emstrur/Botnar Hut	5		www.fi.is +354 568 2533 fi@fi.is
Stage 4b/5a Langidalur Hut	6		www.fi.is +354 568 2533 fi@fi.is
Stage v4b/v4c (1.7km OR) Volcano Huts, Húsadalur	7	No utensils in kitchen	www.volcanotrails.com +354 419 4000 info@volcanotrails.is
Stage 5a/5b Básar Hut	8		www.utivist.is www.nat.is www.basarcabins.is +354 893 2910 info@basarcabins.com
Stage 5b/6a (0.7km OR) Fimmvörðuháls/ Fimmvörðuskáli Hut	9		www.utivist.is +354 562 1000 utivist@utivist.is
Stage 6a/6b Baldvinsskáli Hut	10		www.fi.is +354 568 2533 fi@fi.is
Stage 6b Skógar Camping Ground	11		www.ferdalaq.is +354 863 8064 +354 487 8892 dalur@emax.is
Stage 6b Hotel Skógafoss	12		www.hotelskogafoss.is +354 487 8780 info@hotelskogafoss.is

Fimmvörðuháls Hut (Stage 5b/6a; OR)

23

Facilities

Stage	Place	Private Rooms	Hut Dormitory	Camping	Food/ Drinks	Supplies	Transport
1	Landmannalaugar		🏠	⛺	🥤 ☕	🛒	🚌
1/2	Hrafntinnusker		🏠	⛺	🥤	🛍️	
2/3a	Álftavatn		🏠	⛺	🥤 🍔 🍴	🛍️	
3a/3b	Hvanngil		🏠	⛺	🥤	🛍️	
3b/4a	Emstrur/Botnar		🏠	⛺	🥤	🛍️	
4b/5a	Þórsmörk (Langidalur)		🏠	⛺	🥤	🛍️	🚌
v4b/v4c (1.7km OR)	Húsadalur	🛏️	🏠	⛺	🥤 ☕ 🍔 🍴		🚌
5a/5b	Básar		🏠	⛺	🥤 ☕ 🍔 🍴		🚌
5b/6a (0.7km OR)	Fimmvörðuháls		🏠	⛺			
6a/6b	Baldvinsskáli		🏠	⛺			
6b	Skógar	🛏️		⛺	🥤 ☕ 🍔 🍴		🚌

Food

Mountain Mall Grocery Store & Coffee House at Landmannalaugar (Stage 1)

The huts do not provide meals and there are only three places along/near the LT/FT where you can buy a hot meal:

- ▶ **Álftavatn (Stage 2/3a):** restaurant serving drinks and a couple of simple dishes (12:00 to 23:00)

- ▶ **Húsadalur (Stage v4b/v4c: 1.7km OR):** LavaGrill Restaurant & Bar (breakfast/lunch/picnic/dinner; open to non-residents)

- ▶ **Skógar (Stage 6b):** Hotel Skógafoss Bistro Bar (breakfast/lunch/dinner; open to non-residents); Mia's Country Van Fish & Chips (takeaway); Café Skógar at Skógar Museum

Elsewhere, both campers and those staying in the huts have no option but to cook their own food (unless you have a guide who will do this for you as part of a guided tour package). And because restaurant meals at the three locations above are expensive, most people still prefer to cook their own meals at those locations.

All huts have kitchens with gas stoves/pots/utensils/washing-up liquid: accordingly, if you are staying in huts every night then you will not need to carry these items. However, those camping at a hut are not permitted to use that hut's kitchen facilities and will need to bring their own stoves/gas/pots/utensils. Even if you are only going to camp one night, you will need your own cook-set for that night.

At Landmannalaugar (the N trail-head), the Mountain Mall Grocery Store & Coffee House is located in a green bus. It opens at 10:00 and does not close until late in the evening. It sells drinks, sandwiches, food, gas and basic camping equipment: the range of groceries available is pretty broad (see image on p26). However, at the other huts on the LT, you can only buy basic provisions: gas canisters, freeze-dried backpacking meals, candy, beer and sodas are usually available. Stocks can vary during the season and may run out so we would not recommend that you rely on these absolutely. It is preferable to be self-sufficient and use hut provisions for emergencies only. In any case, the prices of the items are relatively high because they have to be brought up from the valleys below: a current price list is usually displayed at **www.fi.is**. On the FT, do not expect to find any supplies at all.

Given the high prices, and limited range, of backpacking food available in Iceland, most people start the trek with stocks of food brought from home. There are no restrictions on imports of pre-packed food which does not contain meat, milk or eggs. However, according to the Icelandic Food and Veterinary Authority (**www.mast.is**), food containing animal products (meat, dairy products and eggs):

The small shop at Langidalur Hut (Stage 4b/5a)

▶ may be imported for private consumption from European Economic Area (EEA) countries; and

▶ may **not** be imported for private consumption from countries outside the EEA (regulation 1251/2019).

This does not apply to uncooked meat, uncooked milk products or uncooked eggs, the import of which is prohibited in all cases. However, it does mean that visitors arriving from the EEA are permitted to import backpacking meals containing cooked meat, milk or eggs for personal consumption. If you are arriving from a non-EEA country, then perhaps it would be prudent to pack only food without animal products. UK travellers should remember that, after Brexit, the UK is no longer a member of the EEA.

The LT/FT is a relatively short trail so it is perfectly possible to start the trek carrying all the food you will require for the full distance. However, you should choose your food items carefully to ensure that your pack is not too heavy: we cannot emphasise this enough. If you choose food which is too heavy then you may exhaust yourself in the early stages of the trek because your pack will be too heavy. Water is food's heaviest component and therefore most people carry dried food like pasta or rice. Freeze-dried meals for backpackers are the best choice because they are light and are prepared simply by adding boiling water: you can eat them directly out of the bag so there is no washing-up. These days, there are some very tasty meals available from companies like Real Turmat and Firepot. Canned food is not such a good choice as it usually has a high water content and is therefore heavy.

If your budget allows it, you could lighten your load slightly by taking advantage of one or more of the restaurants. Make this decision before you start the trek so that you do not carry food that you will not ultimately use. If you eat dinner at the restaurant at Álftavatn, for example, you will have one less dinner to carry. And if you stay at the Volcano Huts at

Mountain Mall Grocery Store & Coffee House at Landmannalaugar (Stage 1)

Húsadalur (Stage v4b/v4c; 1.7km OR), instead of Langidalur Hut at Þórsmörk, you can eat dinner and breakfast at its restaurant: another two meals that you do not need to carry.

How much food do I need?

According to the National Health Service (NHS) in the UK, the recommended daily calorie intake is 2,000 calories for women and 2,500 for men. As you will be expending a lot of energy hiking and keeping warm, it seems sensible to increase this slightly: perhaps a minimum of 2,500 for women and 3,000 for men. Of course, every person has a different metabolism and will have different requirements but this is a good starting point. Also bear in mind that your daily requirement will depend on how far you are planning to hike each day: the further you hike, the more energy you will use and the more food you will need. Remember also to bring a little extra food (over and above your estimated daily requirements) for emergencies.

Suggested daily menu

Breakfast: instant porridge is a good option because it is light and packed with calories. You can get a variety of different flavours. It is also cheap and, in many countries, it is available in supermarkets. You prepare it simply by adding hot water. You can also buy pre-packed freeze-dried breakfast meals: although they are convenient, they are more expensive.

Lunch & snacks during the day: nuts are hard to beat as they are light and packed with energy. Peanuts, for example, have more calories per gram than most other foods. Dried fruit is also good and will help keep your bodily functions regular. Energy bars and candy can help to provide some variety.

Dinner: freeze-dried meals are a good choice. Although they can be expensive, the good quality brands make dinner on the trail something to look forward to. Dried pasta and rice are OK too: you can eat these with packet sauces (prepared by adding water).

*Approaching the fumaroles
at Stórihver (Stage 1)*

Travel to Iceland

Keflavík is Iceland's main airport: it is 50km SW of Reykjavík, the capital of Iceland. It has flights to/from a variety of cities in Europe and North America.

Travel between Keflavík Airport and Reykjavík:

Businesses operating buses between Keflavík Airport and Reykjavík include the following:

Flybus (operated by RE) travels between the airport and BSÍ, Reykjavík's city centre bus station. However, you can also request drop-off/pick-up at your Reykjavík hotel/guesthouse/hostel/campsite. The buses take 45min and run regularly during the day, serving every flight. The cost is 3,499/6,499 ISK one-way/return. Tickets are flexible and cancellation is free. RE also sells packages which combine the airport bus with trips to the famous Blue Lagoon thermal baths. Further information/bookings: **www.re.is**; +354 580 5400.

Gray Line operates a similar service to Flybus: **www.grayline.is**; iceland@grayline.is; +354 540 1313.

Stræto, the public bus company, operates bus 55 daily between the airport and BSÍ. It makes a number of stops along the way, taking about 1hr. It departs every 1-2hr: the timetable is displayed at **www.straeto.is**. It is much cheaper than the privately run services but making payment is surprisingly hard for visitors to Iceland: you will need the Klappið app (see Travel around Reykjavík).

Taxis are available from the rank outside the airport: you do not need to book in advance. It costs €90 or more to travel to Reykjavík city centre.

Travel around Reykjavík

Bus: although Reykjavík city centre is small and you can walk between many of the tourist attractions, there is also a comprehensive and efficient network of local buses which travel around the city. The buses are operated by Stræto and are useful if your accommodation is not in the city centre itself or if you need to travel to Mjódd bus station (from which Stræto buses depart for other towns around Iceland, including Skógar).

Stræto's move towards electronic tickets has made the simple task of payment slightly complicated for overseas visitors. The easiest way to pay is to use the Klappið app: you can download it onto your smartphone for free from your normal app store. After signing up and entering credit card details, you can buy fixed-price single tickets on the app: each ticket is good for one short journey. For longer journeys (including trips to/from the airport on bus 55), you will need to buy more than one single ticket. If in doubt, ask the bus driver how many single tickets you need for your journey: they seem to appreciate that this system is a bureaucratic challenge for non-residents and are very helpful. Once you have bought a ticket, it remains in the wallet on the app until you activate it. After activation, a ticket is only valid for 75min so do not activate tickets until you actually need them. After activation, you scan the code when you get onto the bus. The app also has a journey planner which helps you to work out which bus you need: Google maps also assist with this. For further information, see **www.straeto.is**.

Taxi: you cannot hail empty taxis off the street. You either book one in advance or stand at a taxi rank (such as the one at Keflavík Airport). Taxis are not cheap but they usually accept credit cards. Many drivers speak good English.

Reykjavík taxi operators include:

- ▶ BSR: +354 561 0000; www.bsr.is
- ▶ Hreyfill: +354 588 5522; www.hreyfill.is
- ▶ Borgerbílastöðin: +354 552 2440; www.borgarbilastodin.is
- ▶ Airport Taxi: +354 420 1212; www.airporttaxi.is

Travel to/from the trail-heads

There are three primary trail-heads: Landmannalaugar (the N trail-head), Þórsmörk (the middle trail-head) and Skógar (the S trail-head). At Þórsmörk, Langidalur Hut is the official start/finish point of the LT/FT so that is the main pick-up/drop-off location for buses: however, some buses also stop at Volcano Huts (located at Húsadalur, 1.7km OR from Langidalur Hut along Stage v4b/v4c) and/or Básar Hut (2.2km from Langidalur Hut along the route of the FT). The exact trail-head that you need depends upon which trail(s) you wish to walk and your proposed direction of travel: see the table below.

Route	Starting trail-head	Finishing trail-head
LT only (N-S)	Landmannalaugar	Þórsmörk (Langidalur Hut) or Húsadalur (Volcano Huts)
LT only (S-N)	Þórsmörk (Langidalur Hut) or Húsadalur (Volcano Huts)	Landmannalaugar
FT only (N-S)	Þórsmörk (Langidalur Hut) or Básar Hut	Skógar
FT only (S-N)	Skógar	Þórsmörk (Langidalur Hut) or Básar Hut
LT and FT (N-S)	Landmannalaugar	Skógar
FT and LT (S-N)	Skógar	Landmannalaugar

Of the businesses offering transport from Reykjavík to the trail-heads, Trex and Reykjavík Excursions are probably the most popular: we find them to be reliable and efficient. Their prices are similar and you can book both online. Both offer free cancellation (if notified at least 24 hours prior to departure) and free changes to your booking (subject to availability). As well as single fares to the trail-heads, Trex offers a 'Hiker's Bus Pass' for LT/FT hikers which drops you off at one trail-head and picks you up from another: although it is handy to be able to book everything at once, you should bear in mind that Trex's service to/from Skógar is in fact operated by RE so, if Skógar is one of your trail-heads, it can be cheaper to book two separate single fares with RE than to buy Trex's Hiker's Bus Pass.

If you need to pick up supplies before starting the trek, both RE and Trex make a stop at Hella where there is a supermarket and a service station. Usually, there is enough time to use the bathroom and visit the shops but check this in advance with the bus company.

Reykjavík-Landmannalaugar

Bus Company	Reykjavík pick-up/drop-off points	Reykjavík departure times	Landmannalaugar departure times	Duration
RE (Highland Bus)	BSÍ bus station & Reykjavík Campsite	06:30	15:45	4 to 4.75hr
Trex	City Hall & Reykjavík Campsite	07:30 12:30	14:30 18:00	3.75hr

Reykjavík-Þórsmörk area

Bus Company	Reykjavík pick-up/drop-off points	Reykjavík departure times	Þórsmörk area departure times	Duration
RE (Highland Bus)	BSÍ bus station & Reykjavík Campsite	06:30	**Básar/Langidalur/ Húsadalur:** 15:00/15:15/16:00 **Húsadalur/Básar/ Langidalur:** 19:15/20:00/20:15	4 to 5hr
Trex	City Hall & Reykjavík Campsite	07:30 12:30	**Langidalur/Básar:** 14:30/14:45 18:00/18:15	3.75hr

Reykjavík-Skógar: RE runs one bus daily in each direction. Reykjavík to Skógar is fast but Skógar to Reykjavík takes a long time because the bus waits at Hvolsvöllur for 6hrs to connect with RE's bus from Þórsmörk. Stræto's Bus 51 is much quicker between Reykjavík and Skógar: it runs once each day in both directions. It is also cheaper than RE, costing 5880 ISK: you can pay on-board with a contactless credit card/smartphone. The downside is that you cannot book Stræto's bus in advance. Also, its Reykjavík stop is at Mjódd which is 7km from the city centre: one of Stræto's frequent Reykjavík city buses can take you from Mjódd to the city centre but you will need the Klappið app to pay the fare (see Travel around Reykjavík). The app also has a journey planner which will help you decide which bus to take: Google maps also assist with this.

Bus Company	Reykjavík pick-up/drop-off points	Reykjavík departure times	Skógar departure times	Duration
RE (Highland Bus)	BSÍ bus station & Reykjavík Campsite	06:30	10:15	**Reykjavík to Skógar:** 3.25hr **Skógar to Reykjavík:** 9.5hr
Stræto Bus 51	Mjódd	**Weekdays:** 13:00 **Weekends:** 11:30	**Weekdays:** 16:25 **Weekends:** 15:07	2.25-2.45hr

Hvolsvöllur: all buses between Reykjavík and the Þórsmörk/Skógar trail-heads pass through Hvolsvöllur where there are restaurants, a campsite and a gas station. If you are hiking only the FT, you could park a car there and travel by bus to your starting trail-head. At the end of the trek, you could return to Hvolsvöllur by bus and pick up the car. As well as the services referred to above, Southcoast Adventures operates buses between Hvolsvöllur and Þórsmörk/Skógar: see **www.southadventure.is**.

Reykjavík
Keflavík Airport
Hveragerði
Selfoss
Hella
Hvolsvöllur
Landmannalaugar
Laugavegur Trail
Þórsmörk/Húsadalur/Básar
Mýrdalsjökull Glacier
Eyjafjallajökull
Katla
Fimmvörðuháls Trail
Skógar

On the Trail

Costs & budgeting

Although Iceland is an expensive country for overseas visitors, you can hike the LT/FT relatively cheaply. No permits are required to hike and, on the trek, there is little to spend your money on. Because there are so few shops and restaurants along the trail, and because the available food is so limited and so expensive, most trekkers save money by bringing their backpacking food from their home country (where prices are usually cheaper). Furthermore, choosing to camp also helps to keep costs low: the huts are expensive by alpine standards. Other than hut beds, the largest trek-related item of expenditure is transport to/from the trail-heads.

However, away from the trail, costs can quickly mount up. Hotels, food and alcohol are generally expensive but in Reykjavík, prices can be eye-watering.

	Approximate Cost (subject to change)
Room in Reykjavík hotel	From €100 upwards (for 2 people sharing a double/twin room)
Room in Reykjavík guesthouse	From €80 upwards (for 2 people sharing a double/twin room)
Bed in Reykjavík hostel	From €45 upwards
Bed in Laugavegur Hut	€72
Laugavegur campsite	€17 per person
Meal in café/restaurant	€20 upwards (excluding drinks)
Beer (0.5L)	€6-10

At the date of press, €1 was worth around 152 ISK.

Weather

The weather in Iceland is notoriously bad and unpredictable and there are few places where that is more true than in the mountainous terrain of the LT/FT. Even in summer, high winds, heavy rain, low cloud and poor visibility are common: winds can be ferocious, especially near the high points of the trails such as Hrafntinnusker and the Fimmvörðuháls pass; rain can be biblical and relentless; and the cloud can be so thick that the route is hard to follow. Occasionally, it can even snow on the trail. Furthermore, conditions can change very quickly: one minute, you could be enjoying the sun and savouring your good fortune and the next, you could be scrambling for your rain-jacket and cursing your bad luck.

We lead with this cautionary information not to discourage you but to make you aware of the conditions that you might face and to ensure that you carry gear which can cope with them. The good news is that the weather is not always foul. There is plenty of favourable weather for hiking throughout the trekking season (late June to mid-September). Although perfectly clear and sunny days are relatively infrequent, they do occur each summer. However, it is more common to experience a mixture of conditions during the day: perhaps some sun and clear skies for a time with cloud and/or rain during other parts of the day. Bear in mind though that, at these northerly latitudes, temperatures are on the cool side even on a fine day: on the high parts of the trail, temperatures above 15°C are not that common and it can be much colder than that.

If you can, obtain a weather forecast on your smartphone before setting out each day: this is easier said than done though because cell coverage is unreliable along the trail. The Icelandic Met Office (IMO), provides national, regional and local forecasts in English at **www.vedur.is**. Although, it does not provide specific forecasts for places on the LT/FT, there are regional forecasts for 'Suðurland' ('South') where the LT/FT is located: to find the correct part of the region on Suðurland's weather map, use the two large glaciers at the SE of the map as reference points. IMO also has a smartphone app which provides, free of charge, regularly updated forecasts.

For a more localised forecast, see **www.belgingur.is**. You will find two maps of Iceland on the site. The first one shows wind and rain forecasts for the whole island. The second map is even more useful: if you click on the green dots, you will find local forecasts: there are forecasts for Landmannalaugar, Hrafntinnusker, Þórsmörk and Steinar (which is near Skógar).

Many other internet sites and apps also provide forecasts, with a varying degree of reliability. If you are unable to obtain a forecast on your smartphone then it is sensible to speak to the hut wardens: their understanding of local weather conditions is often invaluable and you should follow their advice if they tell you it is not safe to hike.

Paths and waymarking

Normally, paths and tracks on the LT are well-defined. On the LT, the terrain undulates regularly and, although gradients are not normally severe, there are some short sections which are very steep. Most paths are well maintained and straightforward to walk upon but occasionally, there are rocky, challenging sections. Some paths can be muddy and slippery after rain. The route crosses a number of rivers at places where there are no bridges: you must remove your footwear and wade across. These crossings can be challenging (and sometimes dangerous), particularly in early season when the level of snow-melt substantially increases the volume of water in the rivers: for further information on river crossings, see p39.

The paths on the FT are often rougher, steeper and more exposed than those on the LT: sometimes the drops are sheer and occasionally, ropes/chains have been fixed to the rocks for safety. The FT is not suitable for those with a fear of heights.

Generally, the route of the LT/FT is well marked and navigation is usually straightforward in good conditions. However, occasionally, there are sections where paths are less easy to follow and navigation is more difficult: for example, where the trail crosses rocky zones. Most key junctions have signposts and along the trail, there are frequent marker posts: usually, the tops are painted red or blue but on the Fimmvörðuháls pass there are also some large yellow markers which stand out against the snow. You will quickly get into a rhythm, looking for the next waymark every time you pass one. In the route descriptions, we do not highlight every junction because the waymarking is so good: generally, we only mention junctions if they are particularly significant or if there are no waymarks. As a rule of thumb, remain on the main path unless instructed otherwise by signs/waymarks on the ground or the maps/route descriptions in this book: however, keep your wits about you because there will of course be the occasional exception to this rule! Also, bear in mind that waymarking is at the mercy of the environment: for example, signs and waymarks are sometimes blown down or destroyed by snow.

On the high points of the LT/FT, snow can remain throughout the trekking season, covering paths and making progress/route-finding more difficult: follow marker posts carefully because they can be hard to spot against the snow. Snow cover is greatest in June and decreases throughout the summer. After the season begins, the trail will become quickly tracked by others ahead of you but always be wary of following someone else's footprints: there is a good chance that they are on the correct path but it is obviously possible that they may have strayed from the trail. Also, remember that any fresh snow will obscure footprints. Furthermore, you should be wary of following footprints across snow bridges (see p41): they tend to weaken over time and, just because the bridge successfully supported the people ahead, does not necessarily mean that it will support you. In particular, there is often snow on the Fimmvörðuháls pass (Stage 5b) and in the Torfajökull Caldera (Sections 1 and 2).

Maps

In this book, we have included 1:40,000 scale maps for the entire LT/FT. Because we were unable to find commercially available maps with sufficient detail for our purposes, we commissioned our own maps: we believe that these are the finest maps available for the LT/FT and they are perfect for planning/navigation. However, we also recommend obtaining our sheet map: *'The Laugavegur Trail & the Fimmvörðuháls Trail'* (ISBN: 9781912933501). It covers the entire trek and can be used seamlessly with this book. The sheet map covers a wider area and makes it easier to plan the trek, navigate in poor conditions and identify peaks along the trail. It is available from **www.knifeedgeoutdoor.com** and other online retailers: it is best to buy it before leaving home, because the map that is most commonly available in Iceland has a much smaller scale and we find it harder to navigate with: Mál og Menning's Sheet 4 (Landmannalaugar, Þórsmörk, Fjallabak) shows the LT at a scale of 1:100,000 and the FT at 1:50,000.

Storing bags

If you wish to spend some time in Reykjavík (or elsewhere) after the trek, then you will probably have additional baggage which you need to store while trekking. Because Reykjavík is situated in-between Keflavík Airport and the trail-heads of the LT/FT, most trekkers spend at least a night there before the trek. Normally, your accommodation in Reykjavík will store your bags until your return: some may charge extra for this so check when booking.

Alternatively, Luggage Lockers provide secure baggage lockers at Keflavík Airport and in various places around Reykjavík itself (including BSÍ bus station and Mjódd bus terminal). The maximum number of days you can store your bags depends upon the locker location: between 3 and 30 days. The price also varies by location. For further information, see **www.luggagelockers.is**.

Another option is to have your surplus luggage (that you are not carrying on the trail) delivered to your finishing trail-head. RE and Trex both provide this service but it is not available for the Skógar trail-head. For further information, see Baggage transfer.

Baggage transfer

Baggage transfer services are available on the LT but not on the FT. Although the LT huts are remote, they can be accessed by 4x4 vehicles along rough tracks: this enables baggage transfer businesses to transport your bags each day to your next overnight stop so that you only need to carry a small day-pack on the trail. This spares you from the burden of having to carry a heavy backpack and enables you to pack more clean clothes and some luxuries.

Most of the companies offering guided and unguided tours will offer baggage transfers as part of the package. In addition, Southcoast Adventure offers a baggage transfer service along the entire LT: there is no need to book a tour to use the service which makes it perfect for independent trekkers. However, it is only available to N-S trekkers starting at Landmannalaugar. The first luggage drop-off point is at Hella where RE/Trex buses stop on the way to Landmannalaugar. Prices start at 10,000 ISK per bag per day. There is free cancellation until 2 days before departure. For further information, see **www.southadventure.is**.

Another option is to have your surplus luggage (that you are not carrying on the trail) transferred to your finishing trail-head. For a small fee, RE can deliver bags to Landmannalaugar or Þórsmörk (Húsadalur, Langidalur or Básar). This means that you would not need to return directly to Reykjavík to collect your clean clothes after the trek. It also enables you to have your clean clothes delivered to Húsadalur (near Þórsmörk) so that you can spend a few nights in the more luxurious Volcano Huts after completing the LT. You do not need to book this service in advance: simply go to the RE desk at BSÍ bus station just before your departure to Landmannalaugar/Þórsmörk, pay for the baggage transfer and give them your surplus bag. The maximum weight of the surplus bag is 10kg. Trex provides a similar service but they only deliver to Þórsmörk (Langidalur or Básar): there is no extra charge for this if you are travelling with them. Neither company offers baggage transfer to Skógar.

For any baggage transfer service, always use a waterproof pack-liner inside the bag to make sure your gear stays dry.

Fuel for camping stoves

Airlines will not permit the transport of fuel so you will need to source it upon arrival, before setting out on the trek. Most gas stations around the country stock fuel for stoves. Standard screw-in gas canisters are widely available because these fit the majority of stoves. Campingaz canisters (pierceable and twist-on), for use with Campingaz stoves, are also available but they are harder to find. White gas/Coleman Fuel is sometimes available too.

There are gas stations at the following locations which are useful to LT/FT trekkers:

▶ **Reykjavik:** 200m W of BSÍ bus station

▶ **Hella:** RE/Trex buses to Landmannalaugar/Þórsmörk/Skógar stop beside the gas station

▶ **Hvolsvöllur:** RE/Trex buses to Þórsmörk/Skógar stop at the N1 gas station

There are also a few outdoor shops in Reykjavík which stock fuel: see below. At Reykjavík's campsite, there is a place where travellers can leave unused items for others to pick up free of charge: you can often find partially-used gas canisters.

The Mountain Mall at Landmannalaugar stocks a variety of cannisters but stocks can vary throughout the season so it is better to buy them before travelling to the trail-head: they usually have standard screw-in gas canisters but stocks of Campinggaz cannisters tend

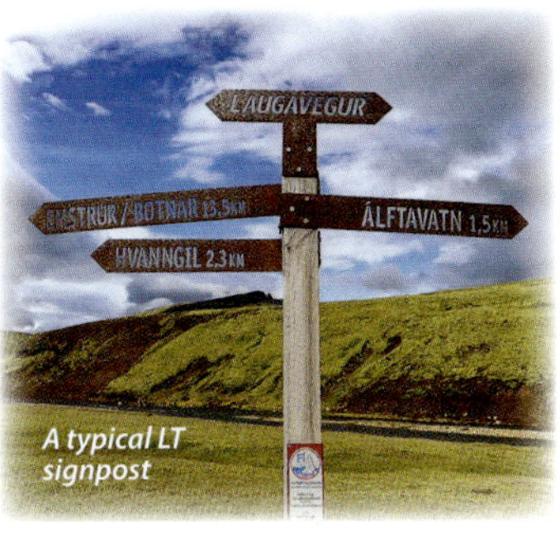

A typical LT signpost

to run out. Sometimes they have fuel for alcohol stoves too. In the communal tent at Landmannalaugar, there is usually a box of partially-used cannisters which you can take (free of charge). At the other huts along the LT, the only fuel reliably available is gas in standard screw-in canisters. On the FT, you are unlikely to be able to buy any fuel at all, although partially-used canisters are sometimes available free of charge at the Fimmvörðuháls hut.

Outdoor shops

The outdoor shops in Reykjavík which sell fuel, outdoor clothing and equipment include:

▶ **Iceland Camping Equipment Rental** (BSÍ bus terminal, Vatnsmýrarvegur 10, 101 Reykjavík; www.iceland-camping-equipment.com)

▶ **Ellingsen** (Fiskislóð, 101 Reykjavík; +354 580 8500; www.ellingsen.is)

▶ **Fjallakofinn** (Hallarmúli 2, 108 Reykjavík; +354 510 9505; www.fjallakofinn.is)

▶ **Everest** (Skeifan, 108 Reykjavík; +354 533 4450; www.everest.is)

▶ **Alparnir** (Skólavörðustígur 10, 105 Reykjavík; www.alparnir.is)

▶ **Alparnir** (Faxafen 12, 108 Reykjavík; +354 534 2727; www.alparnir.is)

You can also rent camping gear at Iceland Camping Equipment Rental (see above) including tents, sleeping bags, sleeping mats, waterproof clothing, gas stoves and backpacks.

Drinking water

Drinking water should be one of your primary considerations each day: even in Iceland, dehydration is a possibility. The water at huts/campsites is drinkable and you can fill up your bottles free of charge each morning before you depart. It is good practice to start the day with at least two litres: that should last most people until they reach the next hut. Plan carefully so that you know where the next hut is: always check your water levels when you pass a hut.

If you do run out, then finding water along the trail is rarely difficult because there are plenty of glacial streams and rivers: remember that the volume of water in streams may vary depending upon the season and the amount of rainfall over previous weeks and months. Although some do it, we would never recommend drinking water from a river, stream or lake, without first dealing with possible contaminants including visible particulates, bacteria, viruses, protozoa (for example, giardia) and parasites. Furthermore, whilst glacial rivers and streams are normally fine to drink from, we would not recommend drinking water found close to geothermal activity (which could be contaminated with sulfur), even after treating it.

It is possible to deal with most contaminants using one or more of the methods described below but you should research thoroughly the specific product you are planning to use to understand its effectiveness and any possible risks:

▶ **Boiling** is the traditional method. A rolling boil of 1min should kill everything in the water. However, it does not remove visible particulates so the boiled water will remain the same colour as when you found it, which can be off-putting. It also uses up a lot of fuel and takes time so is impractical.

▶ **Filtering** usually removes visible particulates, working miracles by turning coloured water clear. It also normally removes around 99.9% of bacteria, protozoa and parasites. Filters are often cheap and light. It is the quickest method of treatment so it is useful for long-distance routes. However, most filters cannot remove viruses (although these are unlikely to be an issue on the LT/FT): if you are concerned about viruses then you will need to invest in one of the more expensive filters that remove them or combine filtering with another method (boiling, UV or chemical treatment).

▶ **Chemical treatment** can remove bacteria, protozoa, viruses and parasites (each product is different so read the labels carefully). However, there are many disadvantages to chemicals: they do not remove visible particulates so the water will remain the same colour as when you found it; water treated with chemicals often has a taste (although you can usually buy different chemicals to deal with that); the water usually cannot be drunk immediately as chemicals take time to kill pathogens; and from a health perspective, consuming chemicals may not be good for you.

▶ **UV treatment** kills bacteria, protozoa, viruses and parasites. However, it does not remove visible particulates so the water will remain the same colour as when you found it: coloured water can be off-putting and the UV treatment is less effective if the water is not completely clear. That said, coloured water is not usually a problem on the LT/FT. The most common products are Steripens which are very light.

Perhaps the best single method for the LT/FT is UV treatment or filtering: because virus contamination is unlikely along the LT/FT, some are prepared to drink water which has only been filtered with a standard filter, running a small risk of virus contamination.

The actual effectiveness of individual products varies and is beyond the scope of this book so do your research beforehand. However, it is worth noting that many products claim to be 99.9% effective indicating that drinking water from wild sources can never be said to be 100% risk free. You will have to weigh up the risks and make up your own mind. You drink the water at your own risk!

If, like many, you do decide to drink from natural sources then, as well as treating the water, there are a few rules that you should follow to reduce further any risk:

▶ Avoid water where there is evidence nearby of animals, especially cows or sheep: carcasses (of dead animals) or faeces can cause contamination

▶ Do not collect water downstream from buildings or grazing areas

▶ Preferably drink from moving water. The faster the better

▶ The bigger the river/stream the better

▶ Generally the higher the altitude the better

	Visible Particulates	Bacteria	Virus	Protozoa	Parasites
Boiling	✗	✓	✓	✓	✓
Filter	✓	✓	Only top of the range filters remove viruses	✓	✓
Chemical Treatment	✗	✓	✓	✓	✓
UV Treatment (such as Steripen)	✗	✓	✓	✓	✓

Ticks

Ticks are present in Iceland although they are rare in the highlands. They can carry Lyme disease or tick-borne encephalitis so check yourself regularly. Remove ticks with a tick removal tool (making sure that you get all of it out) and then disinfect the area.

River crossings

The route crosses five glacial rivers at places where there are no bridges: to continue, you will have to ford them by removing your footwear and wading across. These crossings can be challenging (and sometimes dangerous), particularly in early season when the level of snow-melt substantially increases the volume of water in the rivers. Even relatively shallow water can exert a surprisingly strong pull on your legs, knocking you off your feet.

The river beds are rocky and uneven. Accordingly, crossing in bare feet is not advisable because you will have less stability and are more likely to lose your balance. A fall into the icy glacial water (which is produced by the melting of snow and ice) can be dangerous: hypothermia can quickly set in and, because it can be difficult to remove your pack and get out of the flow, it is possible to drown.

Crossing shoes should be reasonably supportive. Some people wade across in their walking footwear but most prefer to keep these dry and carry specific shoes for river crossings: crocs or sandals are a good choice but flip flops/thongs are not.

The LT's river crossings (N-S):

▶ **Stage 2:** Grashagakvísl River (medium difficulty)

▶ **Stage 3a:** River Bratthálskvísl (medium difficulty; see image on p88)

▶ **Stage 3b:** Bláfjallakvísl River (hard; see image on p117)

▶ **Stage 3b:** unnamed river (easy)

▶ **Stage 4a:** Þröngá River (hard; see image on p42)

How to cross:

Stop: when you arrive at the crossing point, take some time to examine the river before wading in. Do not follow others blindly: try to determine for yourself where the safest place to cross will be. Investigate a little upstream and downstream. Make sure that you know how, and where, you will get out of the water on the far bank.

Wait: if you are hiking alone, or you are concerned about the crossing, then it is sensible to wait until some other people arrive. If something were to go wrong then there would be someone else to assist. You are unlikely to have to wait long: keep your footwear on while you are waiting so that you do not get cold before you start.

Prepare: only start to remove your footwear once others have arrived and you have made a firm decision about where to cross. Quickly remove your socks and shoes. Roll up your trousers. Put on your crossing footwear. Stuff your socks into your boots and tie them carefully to your pack. Put your pack on your shoulders but do not fasten your hip-belt or sternum strap: this makes it easier to remove the pack if you fall into the water. Check your companions' packs to ensure that their boots are properly secured and that their hip belts and sternum straps are unfastened.

Move: only enter the water when you are sure that you and your companions are completely packed up and ready. Once you start, move as quickly as safety permits: the glacial water is ice-cold and will quickly suck the heat out of your body. If the flow is very strong, it can help to face upstream and sidestep across using one pole as support: this helps you to brace against the flow. If you are in a group, it can help to cross together, placing your arms around each other's shoulders for support. Exit the river as soon as you can.

Warm up: it is not uncommon to feel utterly drained after a cold river crossing. Once you and your companions are out of the water, quickly dry your feet and put your socks and hiking shoes back on. It is a good idea to put on additional layers of clothing.

Crossing tips:

▶ Snow/ice melts more quickly during the day than at night. Generally, therefore the flow in glacial rivers increases as the day progresses. Accordingly, it can be sensible to cross earlier in the day.

▶ If it has been raining, then water levels will be higher.

- Do not cross if the water is white: white water is too fast and strong and can pull you in quickly.

- Generally, the narrow parts of a river are deeper and have stronger flow. The wider parts are usually shallower, with weaker flow.

- Be wary of crossing at bends in a river because the depth may not be uniform: it can be much deeper on the outside of the bend.

- Stepping stones: at some crossings, you may be able to walk across the rocks without getting your feet wet. However, be careful not to slip on the smooth surface of the rocks.

- Use at least one trekking pole when crossing. It will significantly aid stability and balance. It also helps you determine the depth of the water ahead. In stronger flow, one pole may actually be easier to handle than two.

- If you suspect that the water may be too high or strong for you then you should not attempt to cross: it is not worth risking your life just to complete the LT.

Snow bridges

On the high parts of the LT/FT, snow melts gradually over the season and snow bridges commonly form over streams. A snow bridge occurs when snow melts under the surface, forming a gap underneath (which is often not visible from above). Sometimes you will be able to see underneath the bridge or spot holes in the snow showing the gap below. However, at other times, there may be no visible signs that the snow has weakened below. If a snow bridge on which you are walking collapses, then you could be seriously injured and, if the flow is strong, pulled under the snow bridge by the current.

If you are crossing a snow-covered stream, then always be aware that there could be a snow bridge beneath the surface. When there is snow on the ground, check the maps so that you know roughly where the streams are located (although smaller streams may not be shown on maps). Listen out for the sound of running water which could alert you to the presence of a stream beneath the snow that you cannot see. Sometimes a long linear groove in the snow can indicate a stream's location.

After the season begins, the trail will quickly become tracked by others ahead of you. However, always be wary of following someone else's footprints across snow bridges: they tend to weaken over time and, just because the bridge successfully supported the party ahead of you, does not necessarily mean that it will support you. Test the ground ahead with a walking pole. If you are concerned, look for a better place to cross. If you do decide to cross, move as quickly as safety allows and do not stop on the bridge.

A weakening snow bridge (Stage 2)

Northern Lights

The Northern Lights (*aurora borealis*) are a spectacular atmospheric phenomenon, lighting up the sky with patterns of colour in high northern latitudes (around the Arctic). There is a similar phenomenon in the Antarctic which is known as *aurora australis*. In simple terms, auroras occur when solar particles collide with the earth's magnetic field, releasing energy in the form of light. They are most clearly seen at night.

The colour of auroras varies depending upon altitude, the composition and density of the atmosphere, and the level of solar energy. Green is the colour most commonly seen from the ground but other colours are possible including pink, red, blue and purple.

Iceland is a very good place to see the Northern Lights but, unfortunately for LT/FT trekkers, they are easier to spot between September and April which is mostly outside the main trekking season. That said, late season trekkers do have a chance of spotting them if it is dark, solar wind activity is strong and there are gaps between the clouds (ideally to the N).

The Þröngá River is usually the deepest and hardest river crossing (Stage 4a)

Equipment

The trekker has no influence over challenges like weather and terrain but can control the contents of a pack carried on the trail. Some trekkers carry only a light day-pack, paying for a baggage transfer service to transport the bulk of their gear to their nightly resting place: see 'Baggage transfer'. Many others, however, elect to carry all their own gear and it is fair to say that a lot of those people set off carrying equipment which is unnecessary or simply too heavy: this can result in injury and/or exhaustion, leading to abandonment. If you are intending to carry your own gear, then you should give equipment choice careful consideration: it will be crucial to your enjoyment of the trek and the likelihood of success.

When undertaking any long-distance route, you should be properly equipped for the worst terrain and the worst weather conditions which you could encounter. On the LT/FT, a key consideration is rain: you might not get any in practice but you should expect it when planning. You should also carry clothing to combat cold: getting cold and wet in the hills is unpleasant and can be dangerous. Furthermore, if you are lucky and the sun does shine, you will want clothing to protect you from it.

However, the dilemma is that you should also consider weight and avoid carrying anything unnecessary. The heavier your pack, the harder the trek will be. A trekker's base weight is the weight of his/her pack, excluding food and water. If you are not carrying camping gear and cooking equipment, it is perfectly possible to get by with a base weight of 5-6kg (13lb) or less. If you intend to carry camping equipment then, by investing in some modern lightweight gear, you could start the trek with a base weight of 8-9kg (17lb) or less. Many people are quick to tell you that the lighter the gear, the greater the price but that is not always the case. While it is true that lightweight gear can be expensive, there are also some excellent lightweight products which are great value. Tents, sleeping bags and backpacks are the three heaviest items that you will carry so they offer the biggest opportunities for weight-saving. But do not ignore the smaller items either as the weight can quickly add up. Accordingly, if you can afford it, it is sensible to invest some money in gear before you leave home. The lighter your gear, the more you will enjoy the trek and the better your chance of success. Be ruthless as every ounce counts.

Recommended basic kit

Layering of clothing is the key to managing body temperature. In cool weather, layers can be added: warm air becomes trapped between the layers, acting as insulation. In warmer weather, you simply remove layers and carry them in your pack. Merino wool or man-made materials are preferable: they are lightweight and warm and they wick moisture away from the skin. Do not wear cotton: it is heavy and it does not dry quickly (making you cold). Always carry a spare set of clothes in case you get wet.

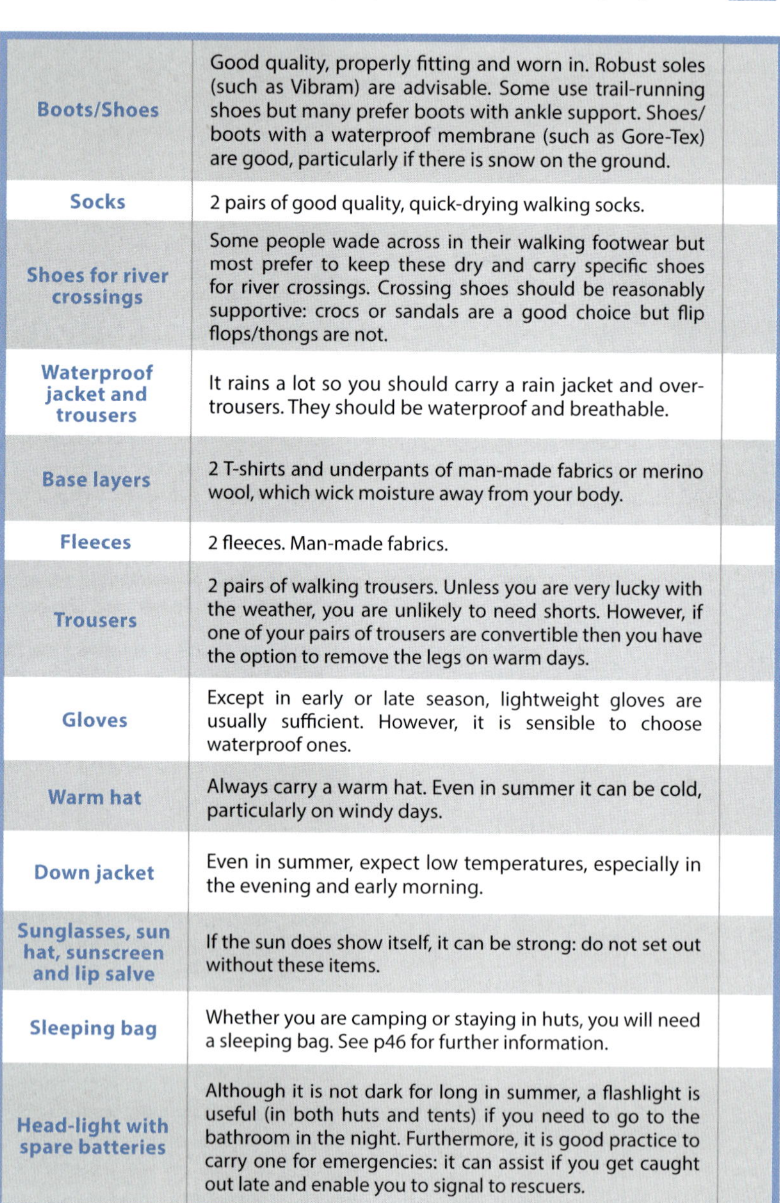

Boots/Shoes	Good quality, properly fitting and worn in. Robust soles (such as Vibram) are advisable. Some use trail-running shoes but many prefer boots with ankle support. Shoes/boots with a waterproof membrane (such as Gore-Tex) are good, particularly if there is snow on the ground.
Socks	2 pairs of good quality, quick-drying walking socks.
Shoes for river crossings	Some people wade across in their walking footwear but most prefer to keep these dry and carry specific shoes for river crossings. Crossing shoes should be reasonably supportive: crocs or sandals are a good choice but flip flops/thongs are not.
Waterproof jacket and trousers	It rains a lot so you should carry a rain jacket and over-trousers. They should be waterproof and breathable.
Base layers	2 T-shirts and underpants of man-made fabrics or merino wool, which wick moisture away from your body.
Fleeces	2 fleeces. Man-made fabrics.
Trousers	2 pairs of walking trousers. Unless you are very lucky with the weather, you are unlikely to need shorts. However, if one of your pairs of trousers are convertible then you have the option to remove the legs on warm days.
Gloves	Except in early or late season, lightweight gloves are usually sufficient. However, it is sensible to choose waterproof ones.
Warm hat	Always carry a warm hat. Even in summer it can be cold, particularly on windy days.
Down jacket	Even in summer, expect low temperatures, especially in the evening and early morning.
Sunglasses, sun hat, sunscreen and lip salve	If the sun does show itself, it can be strong: do not set out without these items.
Sleeping bag	Whether you are camping or staying in huts, you will need a sleeping bag. See p46 for further information.
Head-light with spare batteries	Although it is not dark for long in summer, a flashlight is useful (in both huts and tents) if you need to go to the bathroom in the night. Furthermore, it is good practice to carry one for emergencies: it can assist if you get caught out late and enable you to signal to rescuers.

Backpack	Your backpack is one of the heaviest items that you will carry. The difference in the weights of various packs can be surprisingly large. 35-40 litres should be sufficient if you are not carrying camping gear. 45-60 litres should be adequate for campers. If you need a pack bigger than these then you are most likely carrying too much. Look for well-padded shoulder straps and waist band. Much of the weight of the pack should sit on your hips rather than your shoulders.
Waterproof pack-liner	Most backpacks are not very waterproof. An internal liner will keep your gear dry if it rains. Many trekkers use external pack covers but we do not find them to be very useful: they flap in the wind and, in heavy rain, water still leaks into the pack around the straps (so you need an internal liner anyway).
Basic first-aid kit	Including plasters, a bandage, antiseptic wipes and painkillers. Blister plasters, moleskin padding or tape (such as Leukotape) can be useful to prevent or combat blisters. A tick removal tool or card is also recommended.
Map, compass & GPS device	For maps, see p35. A GPS unit or a smart-phone mapping app is a useful addition but they are no substitute for a map and compass: after all, batteries can run out and electronics can fail.
Walking poles	These transfer weight from your legs onto your arms, keeping you fresher. They also save your knees (particularly on descents) and can reduce the likelihood of falling or twisting an ankle. Poles are invaluable in snowy conditions.
Phone and charging cable	A smartphone is a very useful tool on a trek. It can be used for emergencies. Furthermore, apps for weather, mapping and hotel booking are invaluable. It can also serve as your camera, saving weight.
Ziplock plastic bag	A lightweight way of keeping money and passports dry.
Ear plugs	Useful if staying in huts: you will thank us if someone snores!
Emergency food	Carry some emergency food over and above your planned daily rations. Energy bars, nuts and dried fruit are all good.
Toilet paper and trowel	Bring a backpacking trowel in case nature calls on the trail: bury toilet waste and carry out used toilet paper.
Whistle	For emergencies. Many rucksacks have one incorporated into the sternum strap.
Knife	Such as a Swiss Army knife.
Portable battery pack	Huts do not facilitate the charging of electronic devices although they usually sell portable battery packs. Most people carry their own battery packs: Anker make good ones.
Toiletries	If you wish to take showers, a small hotel-size bottle of shower gel should be enough to last the trek, saving weight. An almost empty toothpaste tube will also save weight. Leave that make-up behind!
Towel	A lightweight trekking towel is a good idea if you wish to take showers.

Sleeping bags

Whether you are camping or staying in huts, you will need a sleeping bag: huts do not provide bedding. Every sleeping bag has a 'comfort rating': this is the lowest temperature at which the standard woman should enjoy a comfortable night's sleep. There is also a 'lower comfort limit' which is for men. That may sound simple but it is not. Although all reputable sleeping bag manufacturers use the same independent standard, the bags are not tested in the same place so there is a lack of consistency amongst ratings. Also, the ratings are designed with an average man and woman in mind, however, every person is different: some people get colder than others and need a warmer bag. The ratings should therefore be used as a guide only and it is wise to choose a bag with a comfort rating which is at least 5°C lower than the night temperatures that you are likely to encounter.

Between the start of July and the middle of August, a bag with a comfort rating between -5°C and 5°C (depending on whether you sleep hot or cold) is normally sufficient to cope with the likely night temperatures. Outside of this period, it can be prudent to go with something a little warmer in case the weather throws a cold spell at you: perhaps a bag with a comfort rating between -10°C and 0°C. It is quite a difficult decision because although you want to be warm at night, you do not want to bring a bag that is much too warm as that would add unnecessary weight to your pack. Generally, the two coldest places to camp are Hrafntinnusker and the Fimmvörðuháls pass (where it can be very cold and windy): if you plan to camp at either of those two places then err on the side of caution.

Unfortunately, with sleeping bags, price tends to be inversely proportional to weight. This is largely because the lightest bags are filled with goose/duck down which is expensive. Synthetic bags are also available but they are much heavier so down is a better choice for trekking. The disadvantage of down bags is that they can lose their warmth if they get wet but that is less likely if you have a good tent and pack liner. Our advice is first to decide what comfort rating you will require. Then choose the lightest bag (with that rating) which you can afford.

Additional gear for campers

Tent: this is one of the heaviest things that you will carry so it provides a big opportunity for weight saving. Some 2-person tents weigh more than 3kg while others weigh less than 0.6kg. The heaviest ones are normally built for extreme winter conditions and are overkill for the normal LT/FT trekking season. Some of the lightest ones, however, may not be sufficiently robust for the LT/FT where strong winds and heavy rain can batter the tent's outer layer: the thin material will also be prone to damage by the rocky ground at the campsites.

Although a few premium brands charge a lot for their products and there are some very expensive tents at the lightest end of the scale, these days there are plenty of mid-weight tents available at reasonable prices. Tents weighing 1 to 1.6kg often strike a good balance between price, longevity and weight. Consider money spent here as an investment in your well-being and enjoyment of one of the world's great trails. Believe us when we say that a few kgs can be the difference between success and failure.

Your tent should be waterproof to ensure that you stay dry during rainy nights. A footprint is a good idea to protect its base: 'footprint' is a trendy, modern word for what used to be known as a groundsheet. Sometimes you can buy footprints specific to your tent model but we prefer to use a sheet of Tyvek which can be cut to size: Tyvek is extremely tough and is cheaper, and normally lighter, than most branded footprints.

Tent pegs: tent weights provided by manufacturers normally exclude the weight of the pegs. The pegs actually provided with tents tend to be quite heavy and many trekkers buy replacement ones which are lighter. Six heavy pegs can weigh as much as 240g while 6 light pegs can weigh as little as 6g. There are many different types available these days and it is important to match the peg with the type of ground they will be used in. The ground on the LT/FT is often hard and rocky and therefore it can be difficult to drive pegs into it. Accordingly, you should opt for strong pegs: titanium ones (which are very light) are a good choice although they can be expensive.

Sleeping mat: this makes it comfortable for you to sleep on the hard ground and insulates you from the ground's cold surface. There are three types: air, self-inflating and closed-cell foam. The advantages and disadvantages of each are set out below. All factors considered, we prefer air mats although the very lightest ones may not be sufficiently warm for some LT/FT trekkers. Thermarest's NeoAir Xlite and NeoAir Xtherm are good choices.

Sleeping mat type	Pros	Cons
Air mats: need to be blown up	Lightest **Very comfortable** Most compact when packed **Thicker: good for side sleepers**	Most expensive **Hard work to inflate** Can be punctured **Less warm than self-inflating**
Self-inflating mats: a combination of air and closed-cell foam. The mat partially inflates itself when the valve is opened	Warmest **Very comfortable** Quite compact **More durable than air mats** Firmness is adjustable by adding air	Heavier **More expensive than closed-cell foam** Can be punctured
Closed-cell foam mats	Light **Least expensive** Most durable **Cannot be punctured**	Not compact: needs to be strapped to the outside of your pack **Least warm** Least comfortable

Pillow: some use rolled-up clothing but we prefer inflatable trekking pillows which only weigh around 50g.

Stove: you should choose a stove that uses a type of fuel which is readily available in Iceland. Airlines do not permit you to carry fuel on planes so, if you are flying to Iceland, you will need to source fuel on arrival. Although white gas/Coleman fuel is sometimes stocked in outdoor shops, these days gas is more widely available (see 'On the Trail'). Most gas stoves are designed to fit generic screw-on canisters which are readily available in Iceland: these stoves are the best choice. Canisters for Campinggaz stoves (which are popular in France) are available too but are harder to find. Multi-fuel stoves that burn petrol and/or diesel are useful but they tend to be heavier, dirtier and more complicated than many gas stoves: the locations of some useful service stations are listed on p37.

Hundreds of different stoves are available, some more complicated than others. Often the lightest ones are the most simple and often the most simple ones are relatively inexpensive. If, like most campers, you will eat dried food such as pasta and rice then your stove will need to do little more than boil water. A basic stove which mounts on top of a gas canister will therefore be adequate: such a stove should also be cheap and lightweight (less than 100g).

Pots: if, like most campers, you eat dried food such as pasta and rice then you will only need one pot which will do little more than boil water. To save weight, go for the smallest pot that you can get away with. For example, if you are travelling solo and planning to use freeze-dried backpacking meals then you would need nothing bigger than a 500-600ml pot. Titanium pots are usually the lightest but they are slightly more expensive. Get the lightest one that you can afford.

Fork/Spoon: we love Sporks! They have a spoon at one end and a fork at the other. They weigh only 9g and cost very little.

Safety

*Mobile bridge across the
Krossá River (Stage 5a)*

The weather in Iceland is notoriously unpredictable. A sudden weather shift or an injury can alter your circumstances dramatically so treat the mountains with respect and be conscious of your experience levels and physical capabilities. The following is a non-exhaustive list of recommendations:

▶ The fitter you are at the start of your trip, the more you will enjoy the hiking.

▶ Start hiking early in the day to allow surplus time in case something goes wrong.

▶ Do not stray from the waymarked paths so as to avoid getting lost or straying into geothermal areas and to help prevent erosion of the landscape.

▶ Before you set out each day, study the route and make plans based upon the abilities of the weakest member of your party.

▶ Obtain a weather forecast (daily if possible) and reassess your plans in light of it. Avoid exposed routes if the weather is uncertain.

▶ Never be too proud to turn back if you find the going too tough or if the weather deteriorates.

▶ Bring a map and compass and know how to use them. GPS devices are useful too, particularly on Stages 1, 2 and 5b where snow can cover the path.

▶ Carry surplus food and clothing for emergencies.

▶ Avoid exposed high ground in a thunderstorm. If you get caught out in one then drop your walking poles and stay away from trees, overhanging rocks, metal structures and caves. Generally accepted advice is to squat on your pack and keep as low as possible.

▶ In snowy conditions, follow markers carefully and do not leave the route. Be wary of following someone else's footprints: there is always a chance that they have strayed from the trail. Always be aware that snow bridges can form (over streams) that are not visible from the surface: follow the advice on p41 and if you have any doubts, do not cross.

▶ Take great care at river crossings: follow the advice on p39 and if you have any doubts, do not cross.

▶ In the event of an accident, move an injured person into a safe place and administer any necessary first-aid. Keep the victim warm. If possible, use your cell-phone to call for help: the emergency number is 112. If you have no signal then send someone to the nearest hut for help.

▶ When cooking on a camping stove, place the stove on the ground. Avoid using it on a picnic table. We have witnessed a trekker knocking over his stove and spilling boiling water on his legs: this is a sure-fire way to end your trek.

General Information

Language: Icelandic is the main language. However, most Icelanders also speak reasonable English.

Charging electronic devices: Northern European 2-pin plugs are used so visitors from outside Northern Europe will need an adapter. FÍ and Utivist huts do not facilitate the charging of electronic devices although usually they sell portable battery packs: most trekkers bring their own portable battery packs. You can charge devices at the privately owned Volcano Huts at Húsadalur (Stage v4b/v4c; 1.7km OR).

Money: the official currency is the Icelandic Króna (ISK). Credit cards are accepted almost everywhere (including at LT huts). Although you are unlikely to need much cash, there are plenty of ATMs in Reykjavík: there are no ATMs on the LT/FT.

Visas: citizens of the UK, EU, EEC, Australia, New Zealand, Canada or the US do not need a visa for short tourist trips to Iceland.

Cell-phones: cell coverage is unreliable on much of the LT/FT. At some of the high points on the trail, you may get a signal but often there will be none. However, you should find a signal on much of Section 6. When network is available, it is likely to be a 4G/5G service, enabling access to the internet from smart-phones.

International dialling codes: the country code for Iceland is +354. There are no area codes.

WiFi: away from the trail, most hotels, guesthouses, hostels and campsites have WiFi. Along the LT/FT, the only place that has WiFi is the privately owned Volcano Huts at Húsadalur (Stage v4b/v4c; 1.7km OR).

Emergencies and rescue: the Icelandic Association for Search and Rescue is run by volunteers and funded mostly from donations. Rescue services are normally free but this may not always cover helicopter evacuation. Accordingly, it is wise to take out your own rescue insurance. The emergency number is 112.

Medical insurance: depending upon your nationality, any required medical treatment in Iceland may not be provided free of charge so it is wise to purchase travel insurance which covers hiking.

Tourist information: the following websites are useful:

► **www.visiticeland.com:** the official tourism website for **Iceland**

► **www.south.is:** the official tourism website for **South Iceland**

► **www.visitreykjavik.is:** the official tourism website for **Reykjavík**

► **www.road.is/www.umferdin.is:** information on **road conditions** which helps you determine whether the road to Landmannalaugar is open

► **www.guidetoiceland.is:** visitor information for **Iceland**

► **www.bluelagoon.com:** Iceland's most famous hot spring complex

Wildlife

In Iceland, there are few wild land mammals and you are unlikely to see any on the LT/FT. The most interesting mammal is the Arctic fox which is a survivor of the last ice age and was the only indigenous land mammal when Iceland was settled in the 9th century. The Arctic fox's coat can change colour with the season: brown in summer and white in winter. Reindeer were introduced from Norway in 1771 and now roam wild in the E of Iceland. There are also mink, rabbits, rats and mice. Cows, sheep and horses are reared domestically. Polar bears occasionally arrive in Iceland on ice-floes (from Greenland): sadly, they are shot because they are a threat to human life.

The sea around Iceland is fed by the Gulf Stream and is rich with marine life. There are dolphins (including orcas) and many species of whales including minke, humpback, sperm and blue whales. Whale watching is excellent during the summer so trekkers can take a tour after the LT/FT. There are plenty of grey and harbour seals around the coast and other seal species are spotted too (harp, bearded, hooded and ringed seals). Walruses were hunted to extinction in the 17th century.

Iceland is also rich in bird-life. Inland, there are ptarmigans, snipes, redwings and golden plovers. The coast is teeming with North Atlantic puffins (around 60% of the world's population). There are also gannets, guillemots, fulmars, gulls, auks, skuas, kittiwakes, razorbills, Arctic terns and oystercatchers. Birds of prey include gyrfalcons and sea eagles. Iceland also has many species of duck including the eider duck: in breeding season, the females shed some down after laying eggs and farmers collect it to fill pillows and quilts.

Plants and Flowers

Iceland is well-known for its starkly beautiful and barren landscapes. As well as vast volcanic deserts and lava fields, there is bogland, moorland and grassland. Only 25% of the island is vegetated and the plants that exist tend to be low-growing species. In fact, Iceland only has around 500 species of indigenous vascular plants which is far less than most other countries.

Although Iceland has very few trees today, it was not always like that. When the Vikings arrived, Iceland was extensively forested (perhaps up to 40% of its surface area). The settlers quickly started cutting down trees for firewood and to make houses and boats. Forests were also cut down to clear land for farming. Within 300 years, most of the country had been cleared of trees. Without tree cover, the surface of the island was eroded by the weather and over-grazing by sheep, preventing forests from regenerating. The situation was exacerbated by subsequent volcanic activity which covered previously fertile areas with lava: although ash-enriched soils are extremely fertile, the parts of the country covered with lava have insufficient quantities of soil to support tree growth.

Any forested areas which now remain are carefully protected. The most common tree is downy birch which is Iceland's only indigenous forest forming tree: they are short and often shaped like shrubs. However, there are also a small number of indigenous rowan and aspen trees in the forests. Both indigenous species and conifers (such as larch and spruce) have been planted in recent times and Iceland's tree cover is now increasing. Nevertheless, LT trekkers heading N-S will not see even a single tree until the shrub-like birch forests around Þórsmörk on Stage 4a.

Although the volcanic terrain of the LT/FT is mostly devoid of tree cover, there are plenty of smaller plants. The stars of the show are the humble green mosses which are the first plants to grow on the dark basalt rock (produced by volcanic eruptions), giving it a beautiful and otherworldly appearance. Moss is a multi-cellular flowerless plant which grows in clumps. In fact, around 460 species of moss have been identified in Iceland: three species of woolly fringed moss are among the island's most common plants. Mosses only grow about 1cm each year.

According to the Iceland Institute of Natural History, more than 800 lichens have been found in Iceland. They are a complex life-form (neither plant nor animal) unlike any other on earth. They are a symbiotic combination of algae and fungus: fungus provides the structure for the algae to live in and the algae provides food for the fungus. A number of lichens commonly grow on the volcanic rock including one known as 'Iceland Moss': despite its name, it is definitely not a moss!

Iceland has plenty of wild-flowers from the white Mountain Avens (which are Iceland's national flower) to the lupins which flower in vivid blue carpets around the country in June. In fact, the lupin is a controversial imposter, having been introduced in the 20th century to tackle erosion and improve soil fertility: it is certainly beautiful but it spreads very quickly and prevents some indigenous plants from recovering.

Although you are unlikely to find large carpets of wild-flowers on the LT/FT, you should spot many small clumps, growing in the most unlikely of places (even in the middle of dry, rocky terrain). At Landmannalaugar, there is plenty of bog cotton. Throughout the trek, you will find moss campion, sea campion and wild thyme. S of Emstrur/Botnar, flowers (including heathers) become more common because the terrain becomes greener and more fertile as you approach Þórsmörk. On the FT, the area around Skógar also hosts many flowers.

Iceland's Volcanoes

Marker cairn with a shiny obsidian rock near Hrafntinnusker (Stage 1)

Iceland is littered with volcanoes, many of which are still highly active. The volcanic activity owes its existence to the island's location on top of the North Atlantic Ridge (which runs for 14,000km along the sea floor), where the Eurasian and North American tectonic plates are being pulled apart: during episodes of separation, magma rises from deep within the earth to shallow depths in the earth's crust and occasionally (every four to five years on average), erupts from Iceland's volcanoes. In fact, most of the ridge's volcanic activity occurs under the sea and Iceland is the only material part of it which lies above sea level: this is probably because Iceland also rests on a geological hotspot which intensifies the volcanic activity initially caused by the separation of the tectonic plates.

Volcanologists divide volcanoes into three loose categories: active, dormant or extinct. Active volcanoes are those that have erupted recently (say in the last 10,000 years!); dormant volcanoes have not erupted recently but may erupt again in the future; extinct volcanoes are not expected to erupt again. Iceland has around 130 volcanoes and incredibly, around 30 of them are active or dormant: 18 have actually erupted in the last 1100 years and a few of them (like Katla and Hekla) still erupt regularly.

There are around 30 different volcanic systems on the island and almost all the different types of volcanic structures can be found including, stratovolcanoes, shield volcanoes and calderas. However, Iceland's volcanoes are relatively unusual in that they are often covered with ice. At first glance, it seems counter-intuitive that so much ice and snow should form at a place where hot lava can emerge but this is explained by Iceland's northerly latitude and the high altitude of some of the volcanoes. It is for this reason that Iceland is nicknamed 'the Land of Fire and Ice'.

There are four active stratovolcanoes in Iceland, including Hekla (a short distance W of Section 1) and Eyjafjallajökull (passed on the FT), and they are all capped by glaciers. There are also active collapse calderas like Torfajökull which you walk through on Section 1 and Katla which you pass on the FT: Katla's huge caldera is covered by the vast Mýrdalsjökull Glacier. When ice-capped volcanoes erupt, the ice melts extremely quickly leading to immense flash floods which can cause devastating damage. In Iceland, such floods are common and are known as 'Jökulhlaups' (see p54).

Seemingly everywhere, Iceland's landscape has been shaped and scarred by volcanic activity, both ancient and recent. Almost all of its bedrock is basalt, formed from lava flows or material ejected from volcanoes. In many places around the island, steam and gases spew from the surface and water bubbles up as hot springs: this is caused by the hot magma which collects a relatively short distance below Iceland's surface, heating the groundwater and neighbouring rocks. This heat is of great benefit to Icelanders because geothermal activity is the source of much of the island's energy. However, the magma can also be a destructive force and residents live each day in the shadow of volcanoes which have the power to cause catastrophic damage and loss of life.

Jökulhlaups

Jökulhlaups are the sudden outburst floods which occur as a result of volcanic activity underneath Iceland's glaciers. They can be created in a number of different ways. The largest floods occur when an erupting volcano beneath a glacier rapidly melts the ice. However, the ice can also be melted at a slower rate by geothermal heat alone (as opposed to an eruption): large quantities of water can accumulate gradually before finally bursting out of the glacier all at once. Geothermally produced Jökulhlaups are usually much smaller than those created by eruptions.

It is estimated that the floods can travel at up to 15 km/hr. The volume of water is so great that the floods can cause devastating damage. For example, it is thought that jökulhlaups created by eruptions of Katla discharge 100,000 to 300,000 m^3 of water per second. To put that into context, the average discharge of the largest river in Iceland is 420 m^3/s and the average discharge of the mighty Amazon is 209,000 m^3/s: this means that the rate of discharge of Katla's jökulhlaups can be 500 times that of Iceland's largest river and similar to that of the world's largest river.

The flood water carries with it large amounts of tephra and eroded earth which accumulate far downstream as huge black deserts known as out-wash plains. The floods are so large that the accumulated material can actually increase Iceland's landmass: for example, the floods caused by the 1918 eruption of Katla created 14km^2 of new land and extended the coastline by many kilometres. The floods damage fertile land, farms and man-made infrastructure (such as bridges, roads and power-lines).

Katla

Katla is the central volcano of the Katla Volcanic System which is one of the most active in Iceland. Its caldera is immense with a maximum diameter of 14km and a surface area of more than 100 km^2: it is the second largest collapse caldera in Iceland (after Torfajökull: see p55). A huge chamber of magma lies a mere 2km below the bottom of the caldera: it is estimated to be at least 5km in diameter and 1km thick.

The volcano and its caldera are almost entirely covered by the Mýrdalsjökull Glacier (Iceland's fourth largest) which itself has a huge surface area of approximately 580 km^2. The maximum altitude of the glacier is around 1490m and the maximum depth of the ice is about 750m. Mýrdalsjökull has a number of glacial out-wash plains including Mýrdalssandur and Sólheimasandur. Jökulhlaups from Katla usually occur only a few hours after an eruption.

Since records began, Katla has been Iceland's third most active volcano (after Hekla and Grimsvötn). On average, it erupts every 40 to 80 years. The last major eruption was in 1918 but it is thought that there were smaller eruptions which did not break the ice in 1955, 1999 and 2011.

The most significant recorded eruption in the Katla Volcanic System happened around 934-938 CE. Known as the Eldgjá eruption, it occurred in a 70km long fissure, part of which is below the Mýrdalsjökull Glacier. It produced a lava flow of 700-800 km^2 which is the most voluminous lava flow in Iceland's recorded history. It flowed S, destroying many settlements.

Just W of Katla is another active volcano, Eyjafjallajökull (see below) which erupted famously in 2010. In the 1,000 years prior to 2010, all three known eruptions of Eyjafjallajökull triggered subsequent Katla eruptions within a few months. Since the 2010 eruption, increased earthquake activity has been recorded but there have been few other indications that Katla might soon erupt. Volcanologists continue to monitor Katla closely.

Eyjafjallajökull

Eyjafjallajökull is a long, flat-topped stratovolcano located just W of the FT. It is 1666m high and is covered by a glacier with a surface area of approximately 80 km^2. Within the cone, there is a small caldera of about 3km in diameter. It has been active for around 800,000 years but erupts infrequently: in the last 1100 years, it has erupted only four times. The last eruption was in 2010 and the ash cloud ejected famously grounded air traffic all over Europe.

The eruption started on 20 March 2010 with an effusive eruption in the Fimmvörðuháls pass between Eyjafjallajökull and Mýrdalsjökull: you cross this pass on the FT. This first eruption ended on 12 April. On 14 April, a second eruption began: it was an explosive eruption beneath the summit ice field. The magma melted its way through 250m of ice and the resulting eruption column was 11km high. The second eruption continued until 22 May. The overall volume of eruptive materials produced by the eruptions was, in fact, relatively small but the volume of ash produced was large relative to the size of the eruption. Although a lot of the ash was deposited on the nearby slopes, large clouds of ash were carried by the wind all over Europe, disrupting air traffic for up to 5 weeks.

Torfajökull

Torfajökull is a rhyolitic stratovolcano. Stages 1 and 2 pass through the Torfajökull Caldera which is the biggest collapse caldera in Iceland and one of the largest volcanoes in the world: it is 18km long and 12km wide, stretching all the way from Suðurnámur (NW of Landmannalaugar) to Jökultungur (N of Álftavatn). It is thought that the caldera was created in stages by a series of explosive eruptions and subsequent collapses: the first collapse occurred around 600,000 years ago. The caldera has the largest expanse of rhyolite in Iceland and is one of Iceland's largest geothermal areas with plenty of fumaroles, hot springs and steaming mud pools.

Torfajökull was a sub-glacial volcano, originally covered with snow and ice which ensured that lava from eruptions tended to cool quickly. Only a small glacial area remains today (at the SE edge of the caldera) which is passed on Stage 2.

The grey, pink and orange colours of the landscape within the caldera are the result of the oxidation of substances within the rock. The last effusive eruption was in 1477 which produced the Laugahraun lava fields that you will walk through just W of Landmannalaugar. Laugahraun is mostly a mixture of rhyolite and glassy obsidian but there is also matt black basalt rock.

Glossary of Volcanic Terms

Active volcano: a volcano that has erupted recently (say in the last 10,000 years!).

Ash: pyroclastic rocks which are less than 2mm in diameter. It forms from magma ejected from a volcano. Due to its small size, it can travel a long way from the volcano.

Basalt: a fine-grained igneous rock which is dark in colour. It is formed by the rapid cooling of lava with a high magnesium and iron content. Basalt lava is low in silica and aluminium and is therefore quite runny: as a result, basalt lava flows often move rapidly and can spread over large areas before solidifying. More than 50% of the earth's surface is basalt. On the LT, much of the rock S of the Torfajökull Caldera is basalt.

Caldera or collapse caldera: a circular depression formed after large volcanic eruptions. When huge volumes of magma erupt over a short space of time (emptying the magma chambers below the surface), the ground can collapse into the void created below, leaving a huge crater at the surface. The formation of a caldera is a very rare event. Caldera volcanoes tend to be flat and can be tens of kilometres wide. Gigantic calderas (like Torfajökull) are known as 'super-volcanoes'.

Dormant volcano: a volcano that has not erupted recently but may erupt again in the future.

Effusive eruption: an eruption during which lava flows out of a volcano in a slow and steady fashion.

Explosive eruption: a violent eruption which throws ash and rock fragments into the air. Normally, volcanoes erupt explosively when gases are dissolved in the magma: as the magma rises towards the earth's surface, pressure decreases and the gases expand rapidly. Eventually, the gases escape suddenly, causing an explosion.

Extinct volcano: a volcano that is not expected to erupt again.

Fumarole: a hole from which hot steam and/or other gases escape. The steam forms when groundwater is heated by magma. You will find many fumaroles on Sections 1 and 2.

Geologic rift: a linear zone where the earth's crust is pulled apart by movement of the earth's tectonic plates.

Hotspot: a location where a large plume of magma rises from deep within the earth.

Fumarole (Stage 1)

Hot spring: a place where hot water escapes from the ground. The water is heated by contact with hot rock that has in turn been heated by magma. There is a hot spring at Landmannalaugar (Stage 1) which you can bathe in.

Igneous rock: rock formed from the cooling and solidification of lava or magma.

Jökulhlaup: a melt-water outburst flood caused by geothermal activity or the eruption of glacier-covered volcanoes. See p54.

Lava: magma which has been expelled from the earth's surface during a volcanic eruption.

Lava flow: an outpouring of molten lava which occurs during an effusive eruption.

Lava spire: vertical lava formations caused by the cooling of viscous lava, forced towards the surface during effusive eruptions. Effectively, they consist of lava which has cooled within the 'ducts' of the volcano: years later, as the softer surrounding rock erodes away, the harder rock spires are exposed. The spires are therefore a cast of the volcano's ducts.

Magma: a hot mixture of molten rock, gas and crystals which is trapped underground. Its temperature is usually 800-1,200°C. As soon as magma is expelled from a volcano, it is known as 'lava'.

Mudpot or mud pool: an acidic pool of bubbling mud which forms in areas of volcanic activity where surface water, which has accumulated, cannot run away. Below the ground, steam forms when groundwater is heated by magma. The steam rises towards the surface (together with hydrogen sulfide gas) and heats water which has collected on the surface. The water and hydrogen sulfide mix, producing sulphuric acid. The acid breaks down the neighbouring rock into mud or clay. The mud bubbles because of the continuing supply of rising steam. The hydrogen sulfide often makes mudpots smell of rotten eggs.

Obsidian: a glassy igneous rock which is usually black although red, brown, grey or green obsidian sometimes occur. It forms when lava cools very quickly and is often found at the edges of rhyolitic lava flows. It has a high silica content.

Pyroclastic rocks or tephra: loose deposits of volcanic rock generated by explosive volcanic eruptions. They form from magma ejected from a volcano into the air. Volcanologists classify them according to size: if they are less than 2mm in diameter, they are 'ash' (see above). Rock fragments between 2mm and 64mm, are 'lapilli'. And rocks larger than 64mm are 'volcanic bombs' (see below).

Rhyolite: an igneous rock which forms when magma which is rich in silica cools quickly on the surface. Because the magma is so viscous, it is more often associated with highly explosive eruptions. It is usually light in colour (often cream), however, the presence of Iron Oxide makes it rust brown. The largest expanse of Rhyolite in Iceland is found in the Torfajökull Caldera (Sections 1 and 2).

Rift Valley: a valley formed by a geologic rift. Also see p80.

Shield volcano: a volcano which is very wide but has a comparatively low profile. The shape resembles a warrior's shield. It forms when a central vent erupts runny lava which can travel long distances.

Stratovolcano: a cone-shaped volcano formed when lava flows or pyroclastic rock pile up around the volcano's vent during eruptions. This creates the classic steep-sided shape that one normally associates with volcanoes. They are composed of layers of rock or 'strata' from various eruptions.

Tephra: see 'Pyroclastic rocks'.

Volcano: usually high ground (or a mountain) formed by the eruption of magma from an opening in the earth's crust. The sides of the volcano are usually made of rock formed when lava from earlier eruptions has cooled.

Volcanic bomb: a pyroclastic rock which is larger than 64mm. They form from blobs of magma which have been ejected from a volcano. They are usually round due to the manner in which lava deforms when flying through the air: the surface cools first. However, the exact shape depends upon the amount of cooling that has taken place before the rock slams into the ground.

History of Iceland

Discovery

Iceland was the last country in Europe to be settled by humans and it therefore has no pre-historic period. Nobody is certain when the island was first discovered but some think that the Greeks and Romans were aware of its existence: Roman coins (dating from 300 CE) have been found on the island but these may have been brought over by later visitors. What we do know is that Irish hermits had been living on the island before the Viking settlers arrived. Some of these visitors may have stayed for a while but history has not been generous enough to credit them with settling Iceland for the first time. It is thought that the Vikings first reached the island in the middle of the 9th century: they were Norwegian and one of them, Flóki Vilgerdarson, gave it the name 'Iceland'.

The Age of Settlement (870 to 930 CE)

Around 870, Ingólfur Arnarson and his foster-brother, Hjörleifur Hródmarsson, set sail for Iceland. As they approached the island's shores, Hjörleifur threw overboard some pillars that he had brought from home: he intended to settle where they drifted ashore, leaving the choice of location to the discretion of the Norse gods. The following year, Hjörleifur was killed by his Irish slaves but Ingólfur continued to search for the pillars which were later found on the site of modern-day Reykjavík. the settlement there began around 874 and it is normally thought of as Iceland's first settlement.

The period between 874 and 930 is known as the 'Age of Settlement' because many more people moved to Iceland and settled most of the inhabitable parts of the country. Many were Norsemen, fleeing from warfare and oppression in Norway where King Harald was trying to consolidate power by creating a single state. However, there were also some Christian immigrants. Settlers came in groups, each of which had a chieftain who made the rules for the group: the members of each group usually paid a tax to its chieftain. However, it was quickly realised that it would be preferable to have one law for everyone on the island. Descendants of Ingólfur started to unify small communities around Reykjavík under one assembly. The push for unification spread and in 930 the Icelandic Commonwealth was formed to govern the entire country. It is estimated that the population of Iceland was then around 60,000: a new nation had been created. Although there was a single parliament (the Alþing), there was no common leader and each community had a large degree of autonomy.

The Saga Age (930 to 1030 CE)

Over the next hundred years or so Iceland prospered. Icelanders built homes and some established working farms. Others had boats to fish the rich waters around the island. The Alþing met each summer at Þingvellir, in the open air. This period is known as the 'Saga Age' because most of Iceland's famous sagas relate to heroic events that occurred around this time: the stories were passed on verbally until they were written down in the 12th and 13th centuries.

In 995, Ólaf Tryggvason became King of Norway: after converting many Norwegians to Christianity, he sent missionaries to Iceland. By 1000, the Alþing was split into two factions: Christians and these who still worshipped the old Norse gods. Civil war was averted when the parliament reached a compromise: all Icelanders were to be outwardly Christian but worship of the old gods was permitted in private.

Peace & War (1030 to 1262 CE)

Christianity gradually spread and there was a period of relative peace. However, a small number of individuals gradually grew wealthier and more powerful and by the 13th century, political and economic power was controlled by a few large families. When King Hakon of Norway decided to bring Iceland under his rule, conflict ensued: in 1235, civil war broke out which lasted until the chieftains swore allegiance to the King in 1262. Afterwards, Icelanders had to pay tax to the King and shipping and trade were closely controlled by Norway.

Foreign Rule (1262 to 1904)

Quickly, the power of the King and the church began to grow. The King acquired land in Iceland and introduced new legislation. In 1380, the Kingdom of Denmark inherited Norway and consequently, Iceland fell under the control of the Danish throne. Although the Black Death did not reach Iceland, a similar plague devastated the island between 1402 and 1404, killing at least one third of the population. With fewer people to work the land, many farms fell into disuse and were acquired by the church. A further plague hit Iceland in 1494-95. Volcanic eruptions also harassed the population and destroyed farmland.

Wonderful views on the FT (Stage 5b)

In the 16th century, the effects of the Reformation were felt throughout Iceland: the King forcefully abolished Catholicism and introduced the Lutheran church. Once this had been achieved, the King seized the land and money of the monasteries. Danish exploitation of Iceland accelerated and the King created a monopoly over Icelandic trade which would last for almost 200 years: only certain Danish merchants were permitted to trade in Iceland and they controlled prices, demanding high prices for foreign goods they imported and paying low prices for local Icelandic goods. Although fish, meat and dairy products could be caught or produced locally, grain needed to be imported by sea. Other important goods (such as iron, timber and salt) were also imported. Many Icelanders slid into poverty.

In the second half of the 18th century, natural disasters caused much hardship. From 1752 to 1759, there was a run of bad harvests. To make matters worse, Katla and Hekla erupted in 1755 and 1766 respectively, with serious consequences. Then in 1783-84, the famous Laki eruptions lasted for almost eight months, covering an area of almost 600km^2 with lava: toxic gas poisoned crops and killed animals, farms were destroyed, people were displaced and a famine hit the country. In 1784, there were also a number of major earthquakes. It is estimated that around 10,000 people starved to death. Seeking to help, the King and the Danish government sent food and money. Then in 1787, the trade monopoly was repealed, opening up trade to all subjects of the Danish King.

In 1814, Denmark was punished for supporting Napoleon during the Napoleonic Wars: Norway was taken away from it and granted to Sweden. However, this time Iceland did not follow Norway and remained with Denmark. After the wars, a liberal revolution swept through Europe and Icelanders began to push for self-government. In 1845, a new advisory assembly met for the first time in Reykjavík: it could pass resolutions which the King could then approve or reject. In 1849, a new constitution was introduced in Denmark which removed the King's absolute power. In 1855, Iceland's trade was opened up to the rest of the world. In 1871, the Danish parliament passed a law stating that, although Iceland was part of Denmark, it would have a certain degree of freedom. In 1874, Denmark gave Iceland its own constitution which stated that the Icelandic parliament had legislative and financial power but laws had to be signed by the King: executive power remained with the King but the Royal Governor of Iceland in Reykjavík handled matters on his behalf. For many Icelanders, the constitution was welcomed as a step in the right direction but the movement towards complete independence continued.

Home Rule & Independence (1904 to present day)

In 1904, Denmark granted home rule to Iceland: Hannes Hafstein was appointed Minister for Iceland, taking over affairs from the Royal Governor: executive power finally moved back to Iceland although it was still legally part of Denmark. With its own government sitting in Reykjavík, Iceland now had greater control over its own destiny. The government invested heavily in infrastructure including roads, bridges, hydroelectric power and a gasworks; telegraph links were established with Europe, finally connecting Iceland to the outside world; the fishing industry was mechanised; Reykjavík grew in size.

In 1918, an act of union with Denmark was passed, creating the sovereign Icelandic Kingdom. It made Iceland a free and independent country but the Danish King was still monarch. For the time being, Denmark was still responsible for Iceland's foreign affairs and the supreme court in Copenhagen was Iceland's highest court. Iceland suffered greatly in the Great Depression of the 1930s which caused unemployment and poverty.

During WW2, Iceland remained neutral. When Germany occupied Denmark in 1940, Iceland's parliament decided that the Icelandic government should take charge of foreign policy, supervision of Icelandic waters and all of the King's duties. Because of its mid-Atlantic location, Iceland was strategically important to the allies: if Germany had invaded Iceland, it could have controlled the North Atlantic which was a vital Allied supply link between Europe and North America. Consequently, in May 1940, Britain decided to occupy Iceland itself despite the Icelandic government's protests: the British government promised that it would not meddle in Icelandic affairs and that it would leave as soon as possible. With the influx of troops, Iceland's economy boomed: wages rose as employment was generated by the building of roads, airfields and buildings. In 1941, Iceland agreed that US troops could replace the British and, in return, the USA acknowledged Iceland's independence: in practice, this made the 1918 act of union ineffective. In 1944, the Icelandic parliament formally ruled that the act of union was revoked: this was ratified by a referendum and the Republic of Iceland was proclaimed on 17 June 1944. Foreign control had lasted for 682 years. During WW2, Iceland sustained heavy casualties because Germany sunk many Icelandic ships.

After the war, Iceland joined the United Nations (1946) and NATO (1949). The US troops eventually left but in 1951, during the Korean War, Iceland signed a defence treaty with the USA, allowing the troops to return: the US became responsible for Iceland's military defence and did not withdraw again until 2006.

The Laugavegur Trail

Laugavegur Trail: Landmannalaugar/ Hrafntinnusker

For N-S trekkers, the LT starts with a flourish because you hike what is probably the trek's 'queen stage': many classic images of Iceland come from this part of the route. For S-N trekkers, on the other hand, Stage 1 delivers an epic climax to the trek. In either direction, as you cross the Torfajökull Caldera (one of the world's few super-volcanoes), the evidence of past eruptions is everywhere: lava flows and spires, ash deserts and many different kinds of volcanic rock. However, this is not an extinct volcano and it is sobering to witness the frequent signs of live geothermal activity along the route: steam rises from the ground and there are hot springs, fumaroles and bubbling pools right next to the trail.

However, the most memorable aspect of Stage 1 is the striking and unusual range of colours on display: there is a kaleidoscope of different hues and shades. The yellows, pinks, oranges and browns of the rhyolite rock contrast spectacularly with the bright white of the snow-pack. And the black and grey lava flows are topped with moss of a beautiful and otherworldly shade of green. To fully appreciate this multi-coloured landscape, we highly recommend the short side-trip to the summit of Brennisteinsalda which only adds 15-20min to your day: from there, you can gaze across the caldera and its lava fields. However, the wonderful whale-back ridge that you will walk S of Brennisteinsalda provides the finest views of the day which perhaps epitomise the LT more than any of its other scenery. Low cloud or fog are common so pray for a clear day.

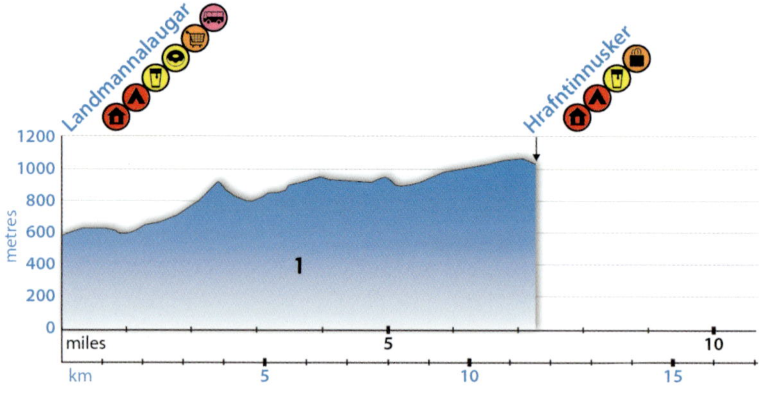

The trek starts at Landmannalaugar Hut which has good facilities, including the best shop on the LT/FT: you can make last-minute purchases before setting out. Many N-S trekkers arrive at Landmannalaugar on a morning bus from Reykjavík and immediately start Stage 1. Before setting out, it is worth taking the time to bathe in Landmannalaugar's hot spring: S-N trekkers will have a muscle-soothing soak to look forward to at the end of the trek. If you arrive on an afternoon bus, you may still be able to walk Stage 1 that evening if you are a fast hiker: at such northerly latitudes, it does not get dark in summer until late. However, you will not have much time to admire the views and, if something goes wrong, there will be less daylight in which to seek help. Towards the end of the season, be aware that there may not be enough daylight to finish before dark. An evening hike is suitable only for experienced hikers and you should not attempt it in bad weather/low visibility.

Hrafntinnusker is famous for its shiny black obsidian rocks and you will find plenty of them on Stage 1 (just N of the hut). The hut/campsite sits at a high altitude and this is not a very welcoming place in bad weather. The wind and cold can make camping hard work and it can be more pleasant to stay in the hut: for this reason, beds sell out quickly so book in advance. If you are only intending to stay in one hut then perhaps this is the one to choose. Confusingly, Hrafntinnusker Hut is also sometimes known as Höskuldsskáli Hut.

As there are plenty of signs and marker posts, route-finding is straightforward in good, snow-free conditions. However, it is fair to say that such perfect conditions are relatively rare. Firstly, large sections of Stage 1 are often covered in snow, even well into the trekking season. Furthermore, the weather in this part of Iceland is notorious: rain is very common but sunny days are not, and low cloud or fog often plague the high parts of the route. When snow-covered, the broad ridges and plateaus can be disorientating particularly, in bad weather or low visibility: this is even more true at the start of the season before the route has been tracked by others or after a fresh fall of snow (which can conceal footprints). Always carry a compass and/or a GPS device. Follow the posts and signs carefully and do not leave the LT route. Drones are prohibited within Fjallabak Nature Reserve.

		Time	Distance	Ascent N-S	Descent N-S
Stage 1	Landmannalaugar/ Hrafntinnusker	4:30(N-S) 4:00(S-N)	11.7km 7.3miles	680m 2231ft	233m 764ft

Accommodation

▶ **Landmannalaugar Hut (Stage 1):** 78 dormitory beds; kitchen with gas stoves/utensils; toilets; showers; hot spring just N of the hut along a board-walk (the hottest water is beside the feeder stream)

▶ **Hrafntinnusker Hut (Stage 1/2):** 52 dormitory beds; kitchen with gas stoves/utensils; toilets; no showers

Camping

▶ **Landmannalaugar (Stage 1):** it is difficult to drive pegs into the hard ground so use rocks to help keep tents in place; large communal tent for cooking/eating

▶ **Hrafntinnusker (Stage 1/2):** the campsite is located below the hut. The ground is hard and snow remains well into the trekking season. Arrive early to bag one of the circular drystone windbreaks which shelter tents from the wind

Take care near fumaroles, hot springs or any place where there is steam/hot water emerging from the ground: never dip your hand into the water to test the temperature (because it is often boiling hot); stay away from steam which is even hotter than boiling water and can cause very severe burns; and never leave the path.

Refreshments/Food

▶ **Landmannalaugar (Stage 1):** Mountain Mall Grocery Store & Coffee House. Open 10:00 to late evening

Supplies

▶ **Landmannalaugar (Stage 1):** Mountain Mall Grocery Store & Coffee House is located in a green bus (drinks/sandwiches/food/gas/basic camping equipment). Open 10:00 to late evening

▶ **Hrafntinnusker (Stage 1/2):** basic supplies at hut

Escape/Access

▶ **Landmannalaugar (Stage 1):** bus

The 'Rainbow Mountains' near Landmannalaugar

Stage 1: Landmannalaugar to Hrafntinnusker

S From the hut's main building, head W ('Hrafntinnusker'). Climb briefly on a path which is often covered with snow. Pass a viewpoint and head W through the **Laugahraun lava fields**: steam rises from the ground a short distance from the path. Pass a series of viewpoints overlooking the lava fields and, to the W, a lovely grassy plain.

1 0:30: Keep SH at a junction ('Hrafntinnusker'). Then start to climb. 10min later, pass through an eerie valley where steam rises from the ground: you can hear water bubbling underground and the air is filled with the smell of sulphur.

2 0:55: TR at a junction with a post: Stages v1a and v1b join from the left. Follow red posts upwards. As you climb, notice the lava spire on the right shaped like a squirrel.

3 1:30: Reach a junction: TR for the short side-trip to the summit of **Brennisteinsalda** (see p72). Alternatively, keep SH to continue on Stage 1: continue following posts up a whale-back ridge, through one of the LT's most colourful landscapes. Often snow lies here late into the trekking season, concealing the path: posts help with navigation and the route is usually well-tracked.

4 2:35: TR at a junction (just below the summit of **Gráskalli**). Follow markers across a broad plateau. Soon, as you descend, notice the steam from the geothermal activity at Stórihver.

5 3:15: At **Stórihver**, pass a bubbling hot spring right beside the path. Soon, reach a junction where there are fumaroles on either side: a short distance E of the junction, there is a large bubbling milky pool. To continue on Stage 1, climb S from the junction: often the route is covered with snow. The landscape becomes less colourful because the rhyolite has been covered with ash from the 2010 Eyjafjallajökull eruption: the white snow and black ash contrast starkly. Follow posts/cairns carefully.

6 4:05: Pass a **memorial cairn** (see p72). There are many shiny obsidian rocks on this section.

F 4:30: Arrive at **Hrafntinnusker Hut (1032m)**.

Stage 1: Hrafntinnusker to Landmannalaugar

F From **Hrafntinnusker Hut**, climb N: often the route is covered with snow. Soon the gradient eases and you head N across a barren plateau: follow posts/cairns carefully. The rhyolite landscape has been covered with ash from the 2010 Eyjafjallajökull eruption: the white snow and black ash contrast starkly. There are some very shiny obsidian rocks on this section.

6 0:25: Continue N past a **memorial cairn** (see p72). Soon, as you descend, notice the steam from the geothermal activity around Stórihver. Later, reach a junction at **Stórihver** where there are fumaroles on either side: a short distance E of the junction, there is a large bubbling milky pool. To continue on Stage 1, continue N from the junction.

5 1:05: Pass a bubbling hot spring right beside the path. Then climb N. Soon follow markers across a broad plateau.

4 1:50: TL at a junction (just below the summit of **Gráskalli**). Follow posts down a whale-back ridge, through one of the LT's most colourful landscapes. Often snow lies here late into the trekking season, concealing the path: posts help with navigation and the route is usually well-tracked.

3 2:45: Reach a junction: TL for the short side-trip to the summit of **Brennisteinsalda** (see p72). Alternatively, keep SH to continue on Stage 1. Follow posts as you descend: notice the lava spire on the left shaped like a squirrel.

2 3:10: TL at a junction with a finger post: the path to the right leads to Landmannalaugar along Stages v1a and v1b. Pass through an eerie valley where steam rises from the ground: you can hear water bubbling underground and the air is filled with the smell of sulphur.

1 3:30: Keep SH at a junction and head N past the **Laugahraun lava fields**. Pass a series of viewpoints overlooking the lava fields and, to the W, a lovely grassy plain. Soon head E through the lava fields. After another viewpoint, descend E.

S 4:00: Arrive at **Landmannalaugar Hut (585m)**.

The rhyolite of the Torfajökull Caldera

Landmannalaugar Variants/Day-walks

Stages v1a and v1b are variants which you can use to travel between Landmannalaugar and **2** as an alternative to the main route of Stage 1. Alternatively, if you had spare time, you could combine the two variants for an excellent circular day-walk from Landmannalaugar.

Stage v1a (Bláhnúkur Variant): see map on p73; orange dotted line

This exciting variant crosses the summit of Bláhnúkur which has incredible views of the Laugahraun lava fields and the rainbow mountains of the Torfajökull Caldera. In good conditions, the amazing views more than justify the extra effort. The path is sometimes steep and unstable with long drops.

N–S: 1.75hr; 4.6km; ascent/descent 408m/298m

Head S from **Landmannalaugar**. TL at a junction. Shortly afterwards, cross a small bridge over the **Brennisteinsöldukvísl River**. Shortly afterwards, TR onto a steep, unstable path climbing the flank of a ridge. TL at the crest of the ridge and follow it upwards. Cross the summit of **Bláhnúkur (945m)** and continue along the ridge. Eventually, the ridge bends to the S. Soon, TR onto a clear path descending initially NW into the valley. Ford the **Brennisteinsöldukvísl River** and continue N into the **Laugahraun lava fields**. At a junction with a signpost, TL and soon reach **2**: alternatively, TR at the junction to return to **Landmannalaugar** on Stage v1b.

S–N: 1.75hr; 4.6km; ascent/descent 298m/408m

TR at **2**. Soon, TR at a junction, heading S. Ford the **Brennisteinsöldukvísl River**. Then climb S on a path. TL at the crest of the ridge and follow it upwards: soon the ridge bends right. Cross the summit of **Bláhnúkur (945m)** and continue along the ridge: soon, descend N. Approaching the bottom of the slope, TR onto a steep, unstable path descending the right flank of the ridge. At the bottom of the slope, TL on a path. Shortly afterwards, cross a small bridge over the **Brennisteinsöldukvísl River**. Then continue N to reach **Landmannalaugar**.

Stage v1a (Grænagil Gorge Variant):
see map on p73; green dotted line

This variant travels between Landmannalaugar and **2**, through Grænagil Gorge. The colours of the rocks are lovely but the views are probably inferior to those on Stages 1 and v1a.

N–S: 0.75hr; 2.1km; ascent/descent 142m/32m

Head S from **Landmannalaugar**. TR at a junction and follow the **Brennisteinsöldukvísl River** along the edge of the **Laugahraun lava field**. Eventually, the path leaves the river and climbs into the lava field. Keep SH at a junction and soon reach **2**.

S–N: 0.75hr; 2.1km; ascent/descent 32m/142m

TR at **2**. Soon, keep SH at a junction, heading NE through the **Laugahraun lava field**. When you meet the **Brennisteinsöldukvísl River**, follow it along the edge of the lava field. The route bends left to head N and leads to **Landmannalaugar**.

Hot spring at Landmannalaugar

Hrafntinnusker Side-trips

Söðull (1132m): see map on p72; orange dotted line

30min (return); 1.8km (return); 109m ascent/descent

If you have time (and energy) to spare when you get to Hrafntinnusker, the short climb to the summit of Söðull is a great way to spend it. It is a spectacular vantage point from which to view the Torfajökull Caldera. From **Hrafntinnusker Hut**, head N along the LT. A few minutes later, TR on a path which climbs NE up the S slopes of **Söðull**. After 15-20min, reach the **summit**. After admiring the views, re-trace your steps back to the hut.

Ice Cave: see map on p72; green dotted line

1.75hr (return); 4.8km (return); 290m ascent/descent

There used to be a beautiful ice cave a few kilometres along the trail that leads W of Hrafntinnusker Hut: unfortunately, it collapsed many years ago. The current lack of ice cave notwithstanding, the wonderful views ensure that the trail itself is still worth hiking. From **Hrafntinnusker Hut**, head N along the LT. A few minutes later, TL on a path heading W along the N side of Hrafntinnusker summit: although you can follow the path all the way to the former location of the **ice cave**, if you just want to appreciate the fine views from the trail then you can turn around much earlier. Afterwards, re-trace your steps back to the hut.

Landmannalaugar Hut seen from the Laugahraun lava fields

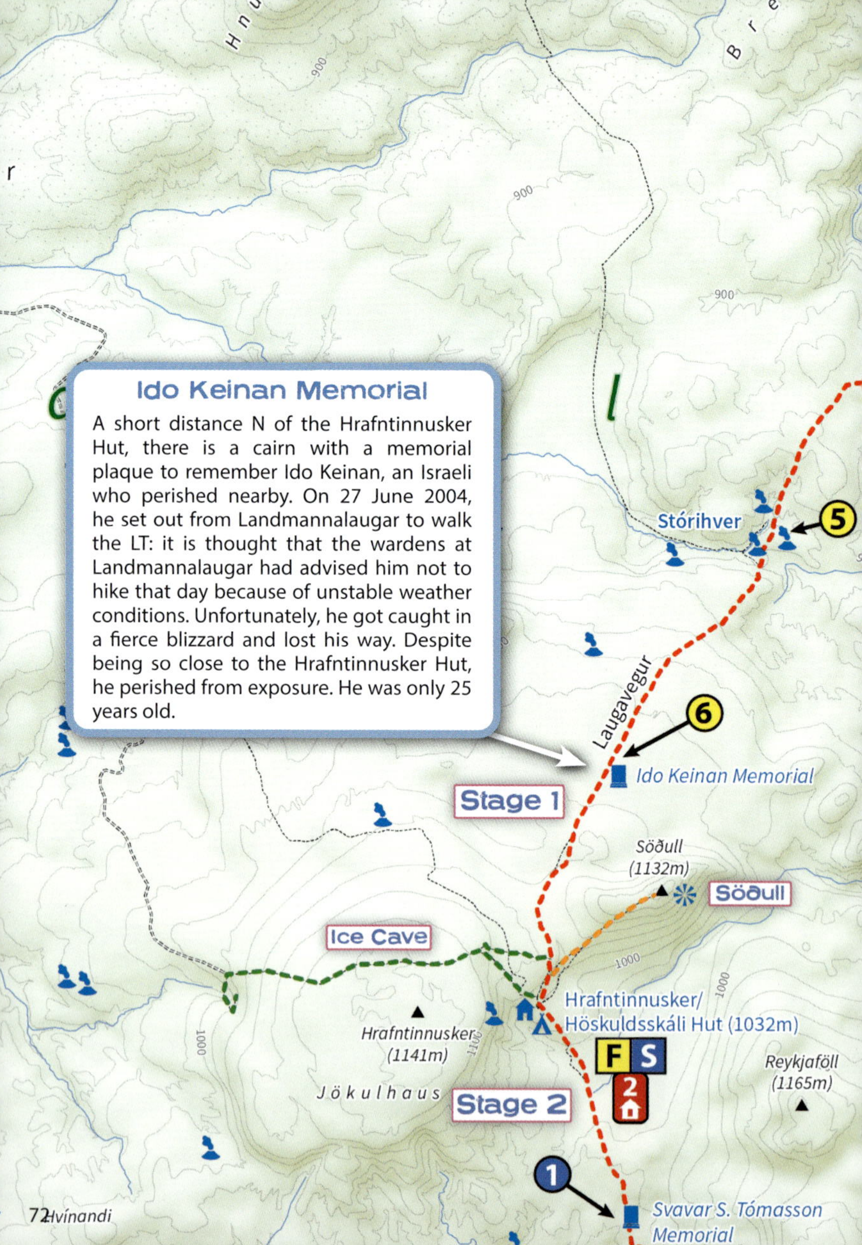

öfðar

Brennisteinsalda side-trip

15-20min return; 50m ascent/descent; green waymarks

From the junction at ③, climb N. 5-10min later, reach the broad summit of **Brennisteinsalda (881m)**. The view from the top is one of the finest on the LT: you can fully appreciate the **Laugahraun lava fields** and the N section of the **Torfajökull Caldera**. To descend, retrace your steps. N-S trekkers do not need to descend all the way back to ③: a couple of other paths soon break away from the Brennisteinsalda main path and join the LT a short distance S of ③.

r

Hnúð
900
900
900

Ido Keinan Memorial

A short distance N of the Hrafntinnusker Hut, there is a cairn with a memorial plaque to remember Ido Keinan, an Israeli who perished nearby. On 27 June 2004, he set out from Landmannalaugar to walk the LT: it is thought that the wardens at Landmannalaugar had advised him not to hike that day because of unstable weather conditions. Unfortunately, he got caught in a fierce blizzard and lost his way. Despite being so close to the Hrafntinnusker Hut, he perished from exposure. He was only 25 years old.

Stórihver
⑤

Laugavegur

⑥
Ido Keinan Memorial

Stage 1

Söðull
(1132m)
Söðull

Ice Cave

Hrafntinnusker/
Höskuldsskáli Hut (1032m)

1000
1000

Hrafntinnusker
(1141m)

Reykjaföll
(1165m)

F S
2

Jökulhaus
Stage 2

1000

①

Svavar S. Tómasson
Memorial

 Hvínandi

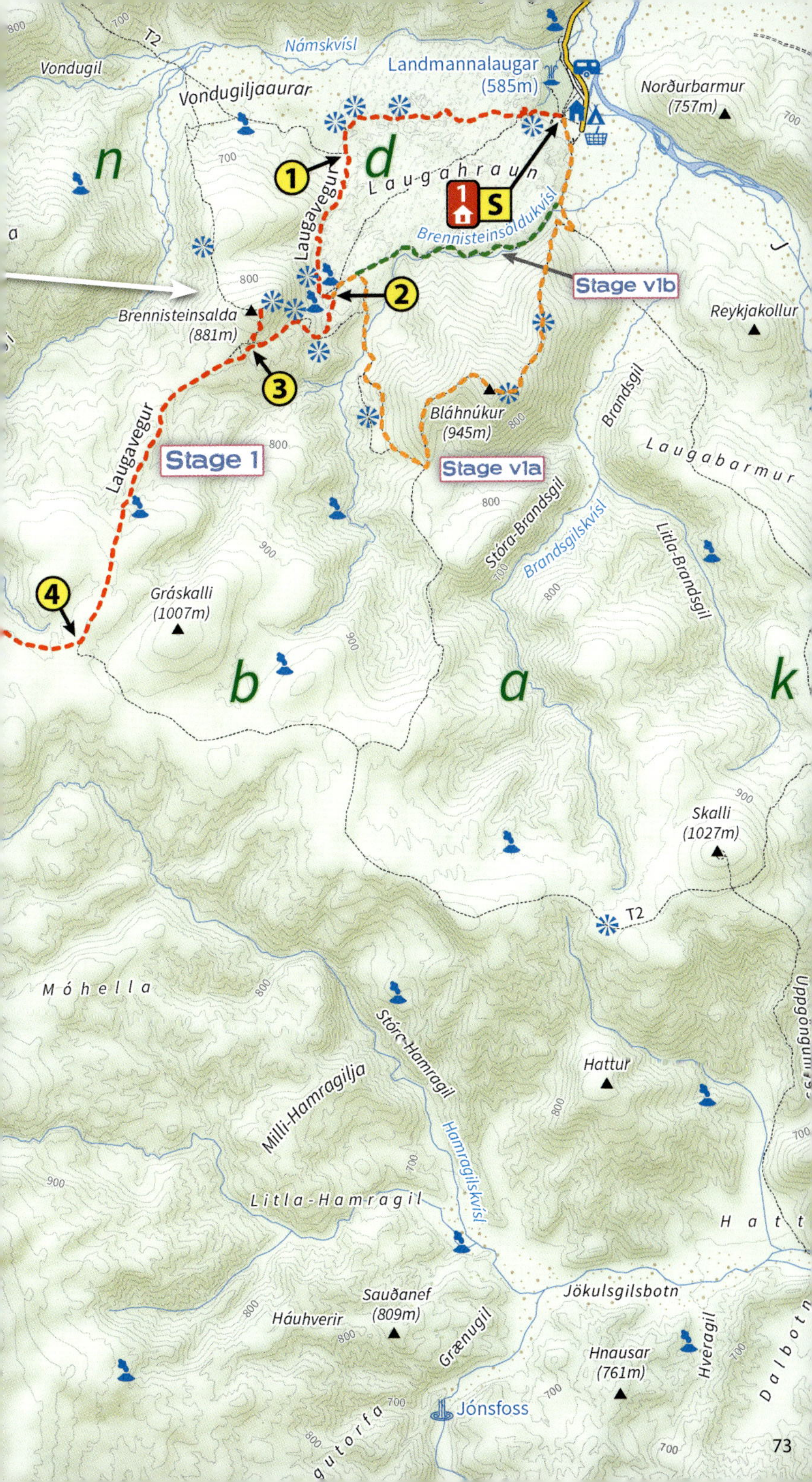

800
700
T2
Vondugil
Námskvísl
Landmannalaugar
(585m)
Vondugiljaaurar
Norðurbarmur
(757m)
700
n
d
700
1
Laugavegur
Laugahraun
2
1 S
Brennisteinsöldukvísl
Stage v1b
a
Reykjakollur
Brennisteinsalda
(881m)
Stage v1a
Bláhnúkur
(945m)
Laugabarmur
3
Brandsgil
Stage 1
Laugavegur
800
Litla-Brandsgil
Stóra-Brandsgil
Brandsgilskvísl
800
700
900
800
4
Gráskalli
(1007m)
b
a
k
900
Skalli
(1027m)
T2
Móhella
800
Hattur
Uppgönguns
800
Milli-Hamragilja
Stóra-Hamragil
700
900
Litla-Hamragil
Hamragilskvísl
Hatt
800
Sauðanef
(809m)
Jökulsgilsbotn
Háuhverir
Hnausar
(761m)
Hveragil
700
Grænugil
700
gutorfa
700
Jónsfoss
Dalbotn
73

2 Laugavegur Trail: Hrafntinnusker/Álftavatn

For N-S trekkers, the journey through the Torfajökull Caldera continues and during the descent from Hrafntinnusker Hut, the sheer scale of it becomes apparent: the vast, barren landscape of bright snow and dark volcanic ash to the S all lies within the caldera and it will be many hours before you exit it. Between the hut and the rim of the caldera, there is plenty more geothermal activity: steam rises from the ground and there are hot springs and fumaroles beside the trail.

The colour of the landscape changes as you progress S: the starkly contrasting black and white patchwork near Hrafntinnusker soon gives way to more of the stunning orange and pink rhyolite that you saw so much of on Stage 1. Then when you finally reach the rim of the caldera, darker colours reassert themselves: black rock coated with deep green mosses. However, it is not just the change in colour that strikes you at the rim's fabulous viewpoints because an entirely new landscape suddenly appears and there is a lot to take in. The magnificent turquoise lake beside Álftavatn Hut catches the eye first: it is set in a rift valley (see p80), surrounded by otherworldly slopes of black and green. If you look closely, you should spot other rift valleys too, all roughly parallel to the Álftavatn valley. You will also marvel at the variety of peaks on display: perhaps the most prominent one is the pointy Stórasúla, to the S of Álftavatn, which dominates so much of Section 3. And, in the distance, you can spot the Mýrdalsjökull and Eyjafjallajökull glaciers, beneath which lie active volcanoes. It is fair to say that this is one of the trek's finest panoramas.

From there, a steep descent leads to the Grashagakvísl River where N-S trekkers will negotiate their first river crossing of the trek: this one rarely causes difficulties. Most

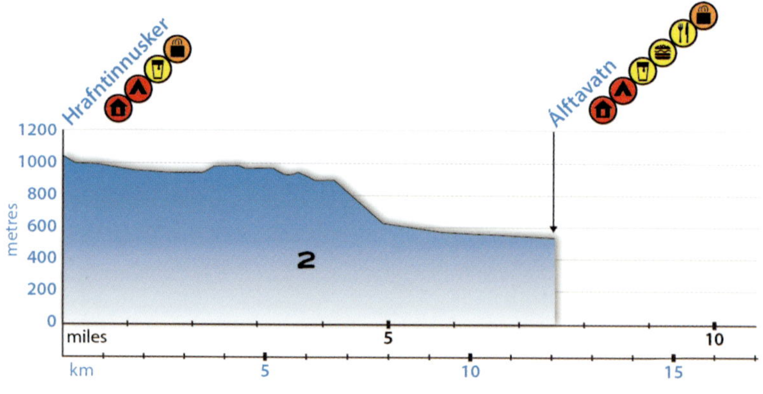

people cross at the point where the path meets the river but there are normally some safe places to cross further upstream too. Normally, the water is no higher than your shins but in early season, and after rain, it can be a little higher. However, often you can cross using rocks as stepping stones without needing to remove your footwear. From the far bank, relatively level terrain leads to Álftavatn.

For S-N trekkers, Stage 2 is an entirely different experience: you leave behind the beautiful black and green terrain and enter the Torfajökull Caldera. At the caldera rim, you witness the wonderfully multi-coloured rhyolite for the first time. Furthermore, although you have been surrounded by volcanoes for the previous few days, Stage 2 marks your first thrilling experience of something hot actually emerging from the ground.

Álftavatn is one of the loveliest overnight stops on the LT. The hut and campsite are beautifully positioned close to the lake which is surrounded by striking black hills decorated with a delicate frosting of green moss. Because of its lower altitude, Álftavatn tends to be less chilly and windy than Hrafntinnusker: however, do not expect a heatwave as the cold and wind can bite here too! Miraculously, there is a tiny restaurant which is a welcome sight in bad weather: the availability of wine and cold beer makes it easy to overlook the fact that its menu is very limited and very expensive. N-S trekkers who are not ready to stop for the day could continue on to Hvanngil Hut (Stage 3a/3b). Most S-N trekkers stop at Hrafntinnusker Hut (see p65) because hiking from Álftavatn to Landmannalaugar in one day is a big ask.

Because Hrafntinnusker is one of the highest points on the LT, Stage 2 is largely downhill for N-S trekkers. It is tougher for S-N trekkers though because they have a steep climb from Álftavatn up to the rim of the caldera: however, S-N trekkers should find the Grashagakvísl River crossing to be straightforward, having already successfully negotiated the deeper rivers further S. The undulating terrain between Hrafntinnusker Hut and ④ is tiring in either direction: there are a series of steep slopes to climb/descend which can be muddy and slippery and there are often snow bridges to cross: take great care and read the advice on p41. Drones are prohibited within Fjallabak Nature Reserve.

		Time	Distance	Ascent N-S	Descent N-S
Stage 2	Hrafntinnusker/ Álftavatn	4:30(N-S) 5:30(S-N)	12.1km 7.5miles	240m 787ft	722m 2369ft

Accommodation

▶ **Hrafntinnusker Hut (Stage 1/2):** 52 dormitory beds; kitchen with gas stoves/utensils; toilets; no showers

▶ **Álftavatn Hut (Stage 2/3a):** 72 dormitory beds; kitchen with gas stoves/utensils; toilets; showers

Camping

▶ **Hrafntinnusker (Stage 1/2):** the campsite is located below the hut. The ground is hard and snow remains well into the trekking season. Arrive early to bag one of the circular drystone windbreaks which shelter tents from the wind

▶ **Álftavatn (Stage 2/3a):** the flat campsite is located on the lake side of the hut

Refreshments/Food

► **Álftavatn (Stage 2/3a):** small restaurant serving drinks and a couple of simple dishes (12:00 to 23:00)

Supplies

► **Hrafntinnusker (Stage 1/2):** basic supplies at hut

► **Álftavatn (Stage 2/3a):** basic supplies at hut

Escape/Access

► **None**

Álftavatn campsite

Stage 2: Hrafntinnusker to Álftavatn

S From **Hrafntinnusker Hut**, follow posts S across a barren landscape of ash and obsidian which is frequently covered with snow. 5min later, cross a couple of small streams.

1 0:25: Pass a **memorial cairn**. There are some fumaroles to the W. The faint path crosses barren ash plains: follow the posts for the best route. Often, there are snow bridges across streams that the route crosses. As you travel S, the colours change: the black/grey ash plains give way to orange and pink rhyolite.

2 2:00: After passing some fumaroles, there are few waymarks. Soon you should catch your first glimpse of the lake at Álftavatn.

3 2:10: Shortly, cross a stream and then climb steeply: notice the blue-grey rocks in this area. The path bends right and undulates along a ridge: the views of the lake are exquisite and **Kaldaklofsjökull Glacier** is just to the E.

4 2:40: Reach the S rim of the **Torfajökull Caldera**. There are some fantastic viewpoints which are great picnic spots on a fine day. Afterwards, zigzag down the steep, rocky slopes: the rock becomes darker in colour again. When you reach the valley floor, follow the **Grashagakvísl River** SW.

5 3:15: Cross the **Grashagakvísl River**, the first river crossing of the LT (see p74). Pick up a path on the other side and head S.

6 4:10: Reach a track. For the **official route**, TL, cross a stream and follow the track all the way to the hut. Alternatively, keep SH across the track and follow a path along the NW side of the stream: in dry conditions, this is more pleasant than walking along the track but you will need to find a way to cross the stream when you approach Álftavatn.

F 4:30: Arrive at **Álftavatn Hut (550m)**.

Take care near fumaroles, hot springs or any place where there is steam/hot water emerging from the ground: never dip your hand into the water to test the temperature (because it is often boiling hot); stay away from steam which is even hotter than boiling water and can cause very severe burns; and never leave the path.

S-N see map on p80

Stage 2: Álftavatn to Hrafntinnusker

F From **Álftavatn Hut**, head NE on a track.

6 0:15: Cross a stream and TR on a path heading N.

5 1:20: Cross the **Grashagakvísl River**, the last river crossing of the LT (see p74). At the other side, TR and head NE on a path, following the river upstream. The climb gets progressively steeper and eventually, the path has to zigzag steeply up the rocky slope.

4 2:35: After a tough climb, the gradient eases as you reach the top of the S rim of the **Torfajökull Caldera**. You will see the caldera's famous orange and pink rhyolite rock up close for the first time. The views back to Álftavatn are exquisite and there are some fantastic picnic spots. Continue NE up a ridge: **Kaldaklofsjökull Glacier** is just to the E. Soon the path bends left and descends steeply: notice the blue-grey rocks in this area.

3 3:05: Cross a stream and then climb.

2 3:20: Pass some fumaroles. As you travel N, the colours change again: the orange and pink rhyolite gives way to black/grey ash fields. For the best route across the barren ash plains, follow posts carefully. There are a series of steep slopes to climb/descend which can be muddy and slippery. Often, there are snow bridges across streams that the route crosses.

1 5:00: Continue N past a **memorial cairn**. There are some fumaroles to the W. Soon cross a couple of small streams. Then climb N, following posts across a barren landscape of ash and obsidian: it is frequently covered by snow.

S 5:30: Arrive at **Hrafntinnusker Hut (1032m)**.

Hrafntinnusker Hut

Hvínandi
Jónsvarða
(1041m)

Rift Valleys

A geologic rift is a linear zone where the earth's crust is pulled apart by movement of tectonic plates. The gap formed by the rift is known as a rift valley. As the earth's crust is pulled apart, the middle of the valley often subsides further, deepening it. In many cases, rift lakes are formed in the valley: Álftavatn is a case in point. Rift valleys are usually long and narrow with level bases. The valley walls are often steep.

900
800
900
800
800
700
900
600
Ljósárgil
Ljósárfoss
Ljósá
Ljósárfoss
600
Ljósárfoss
nfitjarsandur
800
900
800
600
600
Grashagi
Grashagakvísl
5
Stage 2
600
700
Sátubotnar
Torfamýrar
Álftaskarðshryggur
Laugavegur
600
Fjallabaksleið syðri
6
Álftaskarð
Torfakvísl
F 3
S
Lake Loop
Bratthálskvísl
Álftavatn Hut
(550m)
Torfatindar
(818m)
80
700
Álftavatn

Álftavatn Side-trips

Lake Loop: see maps on p80 and 87; green dotted line

1.75hr; 5.5km

From **Álftavatn Hut**, head NW on a path. Ford a few streams. Meet a track at the N tip of the lake: from there, head SW on a path along the lake shore. At the W end of the lake, leave this path and continue anti-clockwise around the lake. The route around the SW and SE sides of the lake is rougher and there are streams to ford. Approaching the campsite, keep to the S side of the stream until you reach a small bridge: TL and cross it. Then follow the LT back to **Álftavatn Hut**.

Bratthals: see maps on p80 and 87; orange dotted line

1.75hr (return); 4.5km (return); 220m ascent/descent

This stunning ridge walk leads to the summit of Bratthals, the prominent peak on the S side of Álftavatn lake. The views of the colourful Torfajökull Caldera are magnificent. The route is rocky and uneven at times. From **Álftavatn Hut**, follow posts E. A few minutes later, use two small footbridges to cross a slow-moving river. Afterwards, TR and head SW alongside the stream. Soon bear left and climb onto the **Bratthals ridge**: follow it SW all the way to the summit of **Bratthals (763m)**. Afterwards, retrace your steps back to **Álftavatn Hut**.

3 Laugavegur Trail: Álftavatn/Emstrur-Botnar

On Section 2, trekkers stand upon the S rim of the Torfajökull Caldera and gaze S across a vast wilderness of black rock and green moss: it is this landscape that you will travel on Section 3. The colours are striking from afar but close-up they are absolutely mesmerising: more careful inspection reveals that the green is not in fact a single shade but rather a mixture of intriguing verdant hues. The effect is further amplified if the sun shines. On Stage 3a, the green is seemingly everywhere and the effect is spectacular. On Stage 3b, however, the colour has been applied more subtly but the outcome is equally beautiful: on their own, the dark, barren plains would be featureless and overbearing but when married with the backdrop of pointy volcanic summits delicately painted with green moss, they are anything but. The colourful volcanoes draw the eye and contrast sublimely with the monochrome basalt.

Although no steam or boiling water gushes from the ground on Section 3, budding volcanologists will still find plenty to pique the interest. For example, just S of Hvanngil Hut, the route leads through a lava flow: although the lava is similar in colour to the obsidian lava at Laugahraun (Stage 1), chemically it is not the same: like much of the rock S of the Torfajökull Caldera, the Hvanngil lava is basalt. Furthermore, on the dark plains of Stage 3b, there are plenty of 'volcanic bombs' which were ejected during previous eruptions of nearby volcanoes. And there are great views of the vast Mýrdalsjökull Glacier which covers the famous Katla volcano and which spans almost the entire distance between Hvanngil (Stage 3a/3b) and Skógar (Stage 6b).

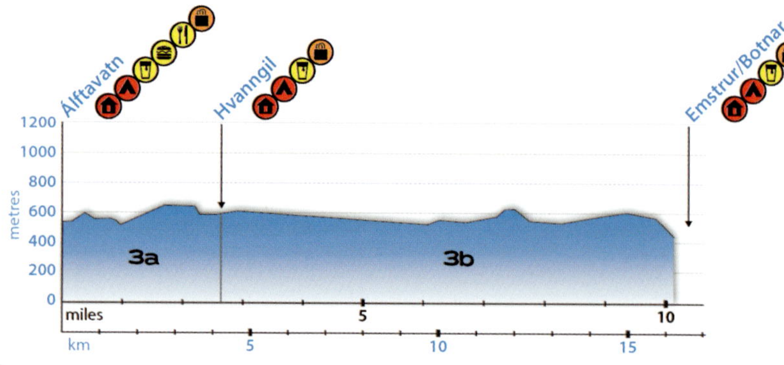

Most N-S trekkers stay at Emstrur/Botnar Hut which has a stunning location within a basalt moonscape, looking onto the Mýrdalsjökull Glacier. The dormitories and kitchens are in three adjacent buildings, each with a balcony where you can sit if the weather permits it. Gas fires are lit inside on cold days. Most S-N trekkers stay at Álftavatn (see p75) because hiking from Emstrur/Botnar to Hrafntinnusker in one day is a big ask.

However, do not overlook the huts/campsites at Hvanngil which are set within a spectacular valley. Although it is usually a more peaceful overnight stop than Álftavatn or Emstrur/Botnar, most people do not even consider staying there which is a shame. The main reason for this is that stopping at Hvanngil can unbalance your itinerary. For most trekkers, the stretch between Hvanngil and Þórsmörk is too long to be comfortably walked in one day and therefore a stop at Emstrur/Botnar is normally necessary: however, the stretch between Hvanngil and Emstrur/Botnar is too short to fill a day and leaves you with a lot of spare time.

Route-finding is straightforward because the entire section uses clear paths which are well marked. The terrain is generally less challenging than the stages further N, except for one (not insignificant) factor: rivers! And there are three of them to cross on Section 3. Firstly, there is the River Bratthálskvísl on Stage 3a (**1**): you will get your feet wet but the water is usually no more than shin deep. The second is the Bláfjallakvísl River (**1**), just S of Hvanngil, which is usually deeper and faster than the rivers crossed further N. It is fairly wide and the water is sometimes knee deep so it is quite a serious undertaking. And it is cold. Very cold. It is not wise to attempt this crossing on your own: solo trekkers should wait for others to arrive before starting across. The third crossing (**3**) is the easiest one and rarely causes problems: depending on the season, you may be able to use the rocks as stepping stones.

		Time	Distance	Ascent N-S	Descent N-S
Stage 3a	Álftavatn/ Hvanngil	1:30	4.2km 2.6miles	154m 505ft	148m 486ft
Stage 3b	Hvanngil/ Emstrur-Botnar	4:15(N-S) 4:30(S-N)	12.2km 7.6miles	196m 643ft	287m 942ft

Accommodation

▶ **Álftavatn Hut (Stage 2/3a):** 72 dormitory beds; kitchen with gas stoves/utensils; toilets; showers

▶ **Hvanngil Hut (Stage 3a/3b):** 60 dormitory beds in the main hut; 20 sleeping spaces in a nearby stable; kitchen with gas stoves/utensils; toilets; showers

▶ **Emstrur/Botnar Hut (Stage 3b/4a):** 60 dormitory beds; kitchens with gas stoves/utensils; toilets; showers

The basalt desert on Stage 3b

Camping

▶ **Álftavatn (Stage 2/3a):** the flat campsite is located on the lake side of the hut

▶ **Hvanngil (Stage 3a/3b):** the camping area beside the main hut (within the lava field) has some sheltered pitches behind rocks. Further away, beside the stable, there is also a second camp-ground which is more exposed

▶ **Emstrur/Botnar (Stage 3b/4a):** there are pitches beside the hut and also along the stream below it. It can be a tight squeeze

Refreshments/Food

▶ **Álftavatn (Stage 2/3a):** small restaurant serving drinks and a couple of simple dishes (12:00 to 23:00)

Supplies

▶ **Álftavatn (Stage 2/3a):** basic supplies at hut

▶ **Hvanngil (Stage 3a/3b):** basic supplies at hut

▶ **Emstrur/Botnar (Stage 3b/4a):** basic supplies at hut

Escape/Access

▶ **None**

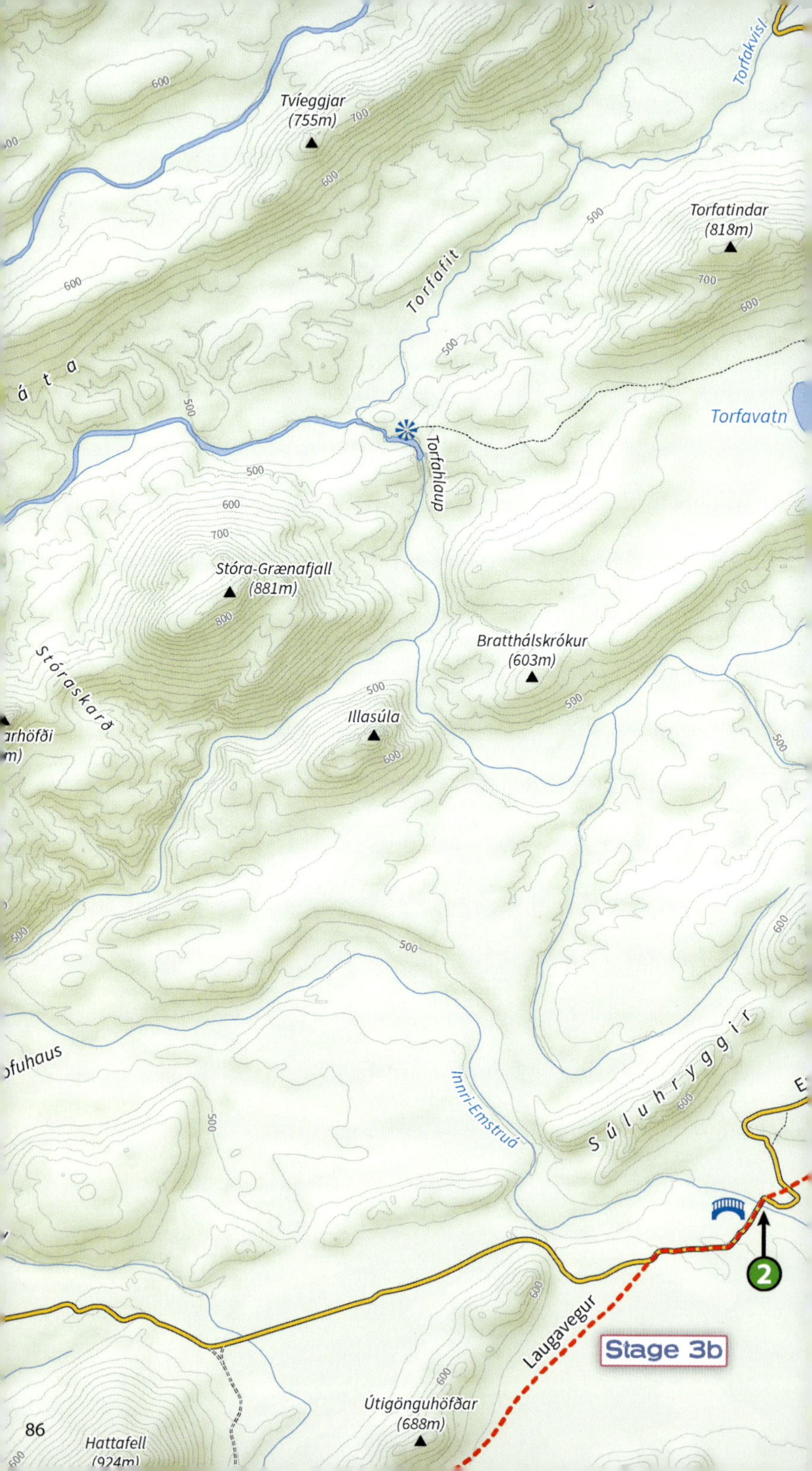

Torfakvísl
Tvíeggjar
(755m)
Torfatindar
(818m)
Torfafit
Torfavatn
Torfahlaup
Stóra-Grænafjall
(881m)
Bratthálskrókur
(603m)
Stóraskarð
Illasúla
...arhöfði
...m)
Súluhryggir
Innri-Emstruá
...ofuhaus
Laugavegur
Stage 3b
2
86
Útigönguhöfðar
(688m)
Hattafell
(924m)
600
700
500
800

Hvanngil Side-trip

Hvanngilshnausar: green dotted line

1-1.5hr (return); 4km (return); 250m ascent/descent

From Hvanngil Hut, head S on a path through black lava flow. Soon TL at a junction, heading SE. Cross a track. Then climb a clear path up the **Hvanngilshnausar ridge**. At the top of the ridge, TL and head N along it: the route is fairly rough. Walk as far along the ridge as you wish and then retrace your steps back to the hut. Alternatively, there is a longer route that descends W to the valley floor and then takes you back to **Hvanngil Hut** along the N side of the river: it is rough and tricky to navigate.

Stage 3a: Álftavatn to Hvanngil

S From **Álftavatn Hut**, head E following posts. A few minutes later, use two small footbridges to cross a slow-moving river. Afterwards, follow a clear path up the mossy slopes: soon head S towards the pointy peak of **Stórasúla**.

1 0:30: Cross the **River Bratthálskvísl**: this is the LT's second crossing and you will need to remove your footwear. Afterwards, follow a clear path across beautiful green slopes.

2 1:10: Keep SH at a junction near the top of a rise, continuing S. There are good views of the **Mýrdalsjökull Glacier** to the S. Soon cross a track. Shortly, at the base of the stunning **Hvanngil Valley**, head S on the track itself.

F 1:30: Shortly afterwards, reach **Hvanngil Hut (556m)**.

Stage 3b: Hvanngil to Emstrur/Botnar

S From **Hvanngil Hut**, head S on a path through black lava flow. 15min from the hut, cross a bridge over the **Kaldaklofskvísl River**. Shortly afterwards, keep SH on a track.

1 0:25: Cross the **Bláfjallakvísl River**, the third river crossing of the LT and the most serious so far (see p83). Afterwards, head SW across a flat basalt plain on a long, straight path which runs parallel to the track. Pass to the S of **Stórasúla**.

2 1:50: Cross a bridge over the **Innri-Emstruá River**. Afterwards, keep SH on a track. 10min later, TL on a path which continues SW across the plains (with spectacular views of the jagged peaks). Pass the magnificent **Stórkonufell** on the left.

3 3:15: In the shadow of the striking summit of **Hattafell**, cross another river: the LT's fourth river crossing is probably the easiest.

4 3:50: Keep SH across a track.

5 4:10: At a junction with a signpost, keep SH (S): the path to the right is the **Markarfljótsgljúfur Canyon Side-trip** (see p90).

F 4:15: Arrive at **Emstrur/Botnar Hut (465m)**.

Crossing the River Bratthálskvísl

S-N see map on p91

Stage 3b: Emstrur/Botnar to Hvanngil

F From **Emstrur/Botnar**, climb NW.

5 0:10: At a junction with a signpost, keep SH (N): the path to the left is the **Markarfljótsgljúfur Canyon Side-trip** (see p90). Cross barren basalt plains littered with volcanic bombs.

4 0:30: Keep SH across a track.

3 1:05: In the shadow of the striking summit of **Hattafell**, cross a river: this is the LT's second river crossing and is probably the easiest. Cross the flanks of **Útigönguhöfðar**. Afterwards, keep SH on a path heading NE across the plains (with spectacular views of the jagged peaks). Pass the magnificent **Stórkonufell** (on your right). TR onto a track.

2 2:30: 10min later, cross a bridge over the **Innri-Emstruá River**. Afterwards, head NE across a flat basalt plain on a long, straight path which runs parallel to the track. Pass to the S of **Stórasúla**, an exquisitely beautiful peak.

1 3:55: Cross the **Bláfjallakvísl River**: this is the third river crossing of the LT (see p83). Afterwards, head NE on a track. Cross a bridge over the **Kaldaklofskvísl River** and continue NE. Head N on a path through black lava flow.

S 4:30: Reach **Hvanngil Hut (556m)**.

Stage 3a: Hvanngil to Álftavatn

F From **Hvanngil Hut**, head N on a track. After a few minutes, TR and leave the track to cross a stream on a small bridge. Then climb NW on a path. Soon, keep SH across the track.

2 0:25: Keep SH at a junction near the top of a rise: continue N across beautiful green slopes. There are good views of the vast **Mýrdalsjökull Glacier** to the S.

1 1:00: Cross the **River Bratthálskvísl**, the LT's fourth river crossing (see p83). Afterwards, follow a clear path across slopes of grass and moss. Eventually, descend towards **Álftavatn Hut**. Use two small footbridges to cross a slow-moving river.

S 1:30: Shortly afterwards, reach **Álftavatn Hut (550m)**.

Emstrur/Botnar Side-trip

Markarfljótsgljúfur Canyon: orange dotted line

1.25hr (return); 3.7km from ⑤ (return); 100m elevation gain/loss

This unmissable short walk leads you along the precipitous cliffs of Markarfljótsgljúfur Canyon. The views are spectacular. The canyon is 200m deep and incredibly, it was created by flood-waters produced by the melting of the Mýrdalsjökull Glacier during an eruption of Katla around 2,000 years ago.

From ⑤, head SW, cross a track and pick up a path heading W (marked with posts). When you reach the cliffs overlooking the canyon, head S along the edge of them: do not get too close to the edge because the ground is prone to collapse and the drops are sheer. The views are incredible. Eventually, reach a fabulous viewpoint at the most westerly point on the cliffs. From there, return to ⑤: either retrace your steps or work your way NE though the interior of the plateau (see map).

Basalt Columns

Basalt is an igneous rock which is formed from the cooling and solidification of molten lava. As the rock cools, it contracts and cracks form across the surface. If the lava is moving, then the cracks are unremarkable. However, if the lava is stationary, columns can form. As the cooling gradually extends inwards from the surface, the contractions continue further and further into the lava and columns are formed. Where the cooling is completely uniform, hexagonal (six-sided) columns are formed. However, where cooling is less uniform, the columns can have between three and twelve sides. Basalt columns are fairly common in Iceland but perhaps the most famous examples in the world are found in Northern Ireland at the magnificent Giant's Causeway which is a UNESCO World Heritage Site: if you are interested in hiking to that geological marvel, then take a look at our book **'Walking Northern Ireland'**.

Laugavegur Trail: Emstrur-Botnar/ Þórsmörk-Langidalur

n the N part of Section 4 there is more of the black desert terrain seen on Stage 3b but the mountain backdrop is different: the peaks are generally broader and less jagged, often forming long ridges. However, further S you will find a few more distinct and unusual summits: chief among them is the mysterious rhinoceros-horned Einhyrningur.

On this part of the LT, you are close to the huge Mýrdalsjökull Glacier which covers Katla, an active volcano: as you cross the basalt plains SE of Emstrur/Botnar, there are great views of the Entujökull Glacier, one of Mýrdalsjökull's enormous limbs. Further S though, the ice-capped Eyjafjallajökull volcano dominates your attention: you can clearly make out the caldera on the summit.

Towards the S end of Section 4, the vegetation gradually changes: grass becomes more common, the variety of plants increases and the shades of green are warmer than those seen further N. You should find plenty of heather and some birch trees (the most northerly ones on the LT) which have managed to take root in sheltered places.

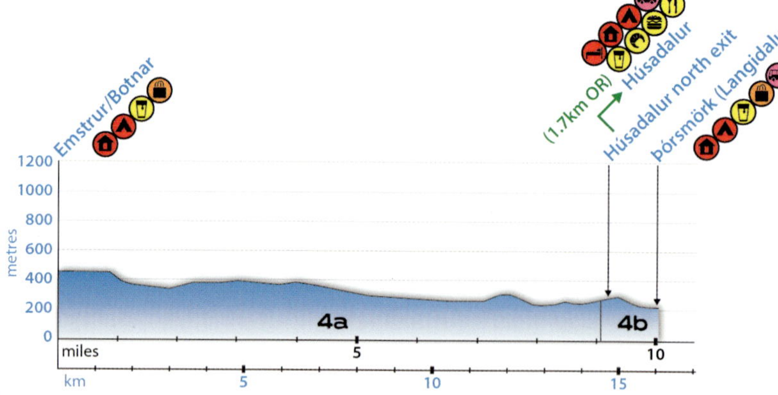

Langidalur Hut at Þórsmörk has a spectacular setting alongside the Krossá River, below the N slopes of Eyjafjallajökull. The camp-ground is particularly beautiful with grassy pitches (a rarity on the LT) although it can be tricky to find a flat spot. Although Langidalur has decent facilities and a basic shop nearby, there are more comprehensive facilities at Volcano Huts at Húsadalur (1.7km OR; Stages v4b/v4c): the latter has a variety of different accommodation options, a restaurant and a hot pool, making it the most luxurious stop on the LT. Buses to/from Reykjavík stop at both Langidalur and Húsadalur (see p30-31).

In good conditions, route-finding is straightforward: paths are usually clearly defined and frequently, there are marker posts for guidance. However, in low visibility, navigation through the flat plains requires slightly more care. Just S of **(1)**, the route is steep and unstable. Furthermore, the paths on either side of the gorge at **(2)** are steep and the drops are sheer: tread carefully and use the ropes/handrails/chains.

Stage 4 incorporates the most difficult, river crossing of the LT. It is wider and normally deeper than the other crossings: sometimes the water can be above knee-height and the pull on your legs is significant. In fact, the river is usually split into sections by gravel bars and therefore you may have to cross a number of channels. Read the advice on p39 carefully.

		Time	Distance	Ascent N-S	Descent N-S
Stage 4a	Emstrur-Botnar/ Húsadalur north exit	5:45(N-S) 6:15(S-N)	14.7km 9.1miles	380m 1247ft	580m 1903ft
Stage 4b	Húsadalur north exit/Þórsmörk (Langidalur)	0:30	1.5km 0.9miles	60m 197ft	100m 328ft

Accommodation

▶ **Emstrur/Botnar Hut (Stage 3b/4a):** 60 dormitory beds; kitchens with gas stoves/utensils; toilets; showers

▶ **Langidalur Hut at Þórsmörk (Stage 4b/5a):** 75 dormitory beds; kitchen with gas stoves/utensils; toilets; showers

▶ **Volcano Huts at Húsadalur (Stage v4b/v4c; 1.7km OR):** glamping tents/private rooms/self-catering cottages/shared dormitories; shared dining area with gas stoves (no utensils); WiFi in main building; sauna/hot pool; showers (free of charge)

Camping

▶ **Emstrur/Botnar (Stage 3b/4a):** there are pitches beside the hut and also along the stream below it. It can be a tight squeeze

▶ **Langidalur Hut at Þórsmörk (Stage 4b/5a):** grassy, sloping campsite beside the hut

▶ **Húsadalur (Stage v4b/v4c; 1.7km OR):** Volcano Huts Campsite; shared dining area with gas stoves (no utensils); WiFi in main building; sauna/hot pool; showers (free of charge)

The rhinoceros-horned Einhyrningur

Refreshments/Food

▶ **Húsadalur (Stage v4b/v4c; 1.7km OR):** LavaGrill Restaurant & Bar (breakfast/lunch/picnic/dinner; open to non-residents)

Supplies

▶ **Emstrur/Botnar (Stage 3b/4a):** basic supplies at hut
▶ **Langidalur Hut at Þórsmörk (Stage 4b/5a):** basic shop (snacks/drinks/freeze-dried meals/gas)

Escape/Access

▶ **Langidalur Hut at Þórsmörk (Stage 4b/5a):** bus
▶ **Húsadalur (Stage v4b/v4c; 1.7km OR):** bus

Einhyrningsflatir
Emstruleið
Stóra
Bæja
Valshamarsgil
Valshamar
Ljósártangi
6
Úthólmar
Litlaland
Loftorfan
Kápurani
Stage 4a
7
Kápa
Tindfjöll Circuit
Systurnar sjö
Hamraskógar
Tindfj
v4b
F S
Húsadalsmoldir
Stage 4b
7
Volcano Huts
v4c
1
400
Húsadalur
Assa
Langidalur
Hut (225m)
Slyppugil
Litlaendahryggur
Litliendi
Langidalur
Stóraendahryggur
Valahnúkur to
Húsadalur
Valahnúkur
(465m)
Stórje
Krossá
Fremra-Sta
F
1
Innra-Engidalsnef
S
Stage 5a
Básar
Fremra-Engidalsnef
6
Stakksflatir
F S
Hvanná
Básar Hut (225m)
Vestrihattur
8
Flár
Stakksgil
Gunnufuð
Nauthillur
Votupallar
Básaskörð
S t a k k h o l t
Merkurtungur
Stakkholtsgjá
(Canyon)
Hátindaflatir
Hátindar
(856m)
Suðurgil
Litlaland
Þvergilsháls
Skaratungur
Steinsholtsjökull
Foss í Stakkholtsgjá
Skaratungnahaus (856m)

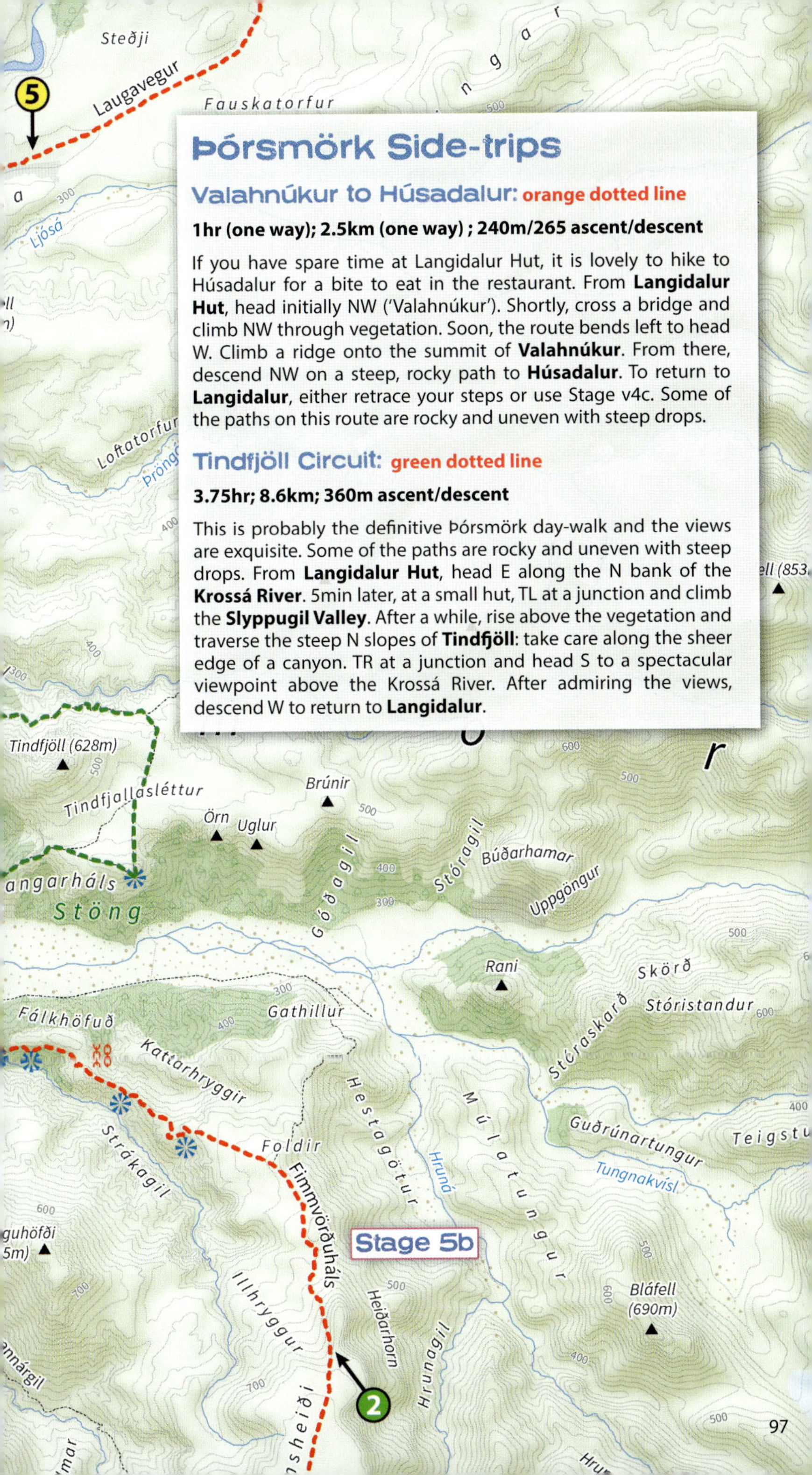

Þórsmörk Side-trips

Valahnúkur to Húsadalur: orange dotted line

1hr (one way); 2.5km (one way) ; 240m/265 ascent/descent

If you have spare time at Langidalur Hut, it is lovely to hike to Húsadalur for a bite to eat in the restaurant. From **Langidalur Hut**, head initially NW ('Valahnúkur'). Shortly, cross a bridge and climb NW through vegetation. Soon, the route bends left to head W. Climb a ridge onto the summit of **Valahnúkur**. From there, descend NW on a steep, rocky path to **Húsadalur**. To return to **Langidalur**, either retrace your steps or use Stage v4c. Some of the paths on this route are rocky and uneven with steep drops.

Tindfjöll Circuit: green dotted line

3.75hr; 8.6km; 360m ascent/descent

This is probably the definitive Þórsmörk day-walk and the views are exquisite. Some of the paths are rocky and uneven with steep drops. From **Langidalur Hut**, head E along the N bank of the **Krossá River**. 5min later, at a small hut, TL at a junction and climb the **Slyppugil Valley**. After a while, rise above the vegetation and traverse the steep N slopes of **Tindfjöll**: take care along the sheer edge of a canyon. TR at a junction and head S to a spectacular viewpoint above the Krossá River. After admiring the views, descend W to return to **Langidalur**.

Stage 4a: Emstrur-Botnar to Húsadalur north exit

S From **Emstrur/Botnar Hut**, descend E into a narrow valley. Pass some tent pitches, cross a stream and climb the other side of the valley. Pass an **information board**. Then head SE across the basalt plains, enjoying views of the **Entujökull Glacier**. 10min later, cross a stream on a footbridge.

1 0:30: Take care descending a steep, sandy slope.

2 0:40: A steep path and metal steps lead down to a bridge over a gorge: ropes/handrails assist with the descent. Cross the bridge: given the huge volume of water being forced down the chasm, this is a thrilling and noisy experience. On the far side, the path is very exposed: there are chains bolted into the rock for safety. After climbing briefly, the path bends right and heads W across another plain, parallel to the river. Later, ford a stream on rocks and then climb.

3 1:25: Reach the top of a ridge where there are cliffs on both sides. There are good views of nearby **basalt columns** (see p91). A short distance OR to the W, there is a viewpoint overlooking **Markarfljótsgljúfur Canyon**. To continue on **Stage 4a**, head SW: cross a rise and then descend. Soon, to the W, the unusually shaped summit of **Einhyrningur** reveals itself. As you continue to descend, the vegetation gradually changes.

4 2:40: Reach a **birch tree**, the most northerly tree on the LT. Afterwards, the path skirts the edges of **Markarfljótsgljúfur Canyon**: take care as the drops are sheer.

5 3:35: The path descends over rocks into a shallow gully which is flanked on one side by short trees. There are interesting layered rock formations on the gully walls.

6 4:20: Cross a bridge over a gorge. Shortly afterwards, climb steeply. Near the top of the slope, bear right and walk along a fabulous ridge. Soon, descend on a clear path towards the **Þröngá River**. At a junction, TL onto a narrow path (no waymark; easy to miss): do not worry if you miss this junction as the two paths soon converge.

7 5:00: Take care crossing the **Þröngá River** (see p93): the LT's fifth and final river crossing is the hardest one. On the other side, it can be difficult to locate the path: it leads you upwards through vegetation.

F 5:45: At a junction (**Húsadalur north exit**), TL for Stage 4b to **Þórsmörk (Langidalur)** or keep SH for Stage v4b to **Húsadalur**.

Stage 4b: Húsadalur north exit to Þórsmörk (Langidalur)

S From the junction, head S on a narrow path through tightly packed vegetation.

1 0:20: TL at a junction: the path to the right leads to **Húsadalur (Stage v4c)**.

F 0:30: Arrive at **Langidalur Hut (225m)** in Þórsmörk.

Eyjafjallajökull seen from near Emstrur/Botnar

Stage 4b: Þórsmörk (Langidalur) to Húsadalur north exit

F From **Langidalur Hut** in **Þórsmörk**, head N on a path.

1 0:15: TR at a junction: the path to the left leads to **Húsadalur (Stage v4c)**.

S 0:30: At a junction (**Húsadalur north exit**), TR for **Stage 4a**. The path joining from the left is **Stage v4b**.

Stage 4a: Húsadalur north exit to Emstrur-Botnar

F From the junction, head NE on a path though vegetation: enjoy it because you will find very few large plants further N.

7 0:35: Take care crossing the **Þröngá River** (see p93): the LT's first river crossing is the hardest one. On the other side, pick up a path climbing NE. Shortly into the climb, TR at a junction onto a narrow path (no waymark; easy to miss): do not worry if you miss this junction as the two paths soon converge. Near the top of the slope, bear right and walk along a fabulous ridge. Soon bear left and descend on a clear path towards the **Ljósá River**: the gradient becomes fairly steep.

6 1:35: Cross a bridge over a gorge. Afterwards, TR and head NE. Walk along a shallow gully which is flanked on one side by short trees: there are interesting layered rock formations on the gully walls.

5 2:15: Climb over rocks out of the gully. The path now ascends gently NE. Skirt the edges of **Markarfljótsgljúfur Canyon**: take care as the cliffs are sheer.

4 3:20: Pass the most northerly tree on the LT. Notice the unusually shaped summit of **Einhyrningur** to the W: it looks like something has taken a huge bite out of it. As you ascend, the vegetation gradually becomes more sparse. Eventually, cross a rise and start to descend.

3 4:40: Reach a viewpoint on the ridge where there are cliffs on both sides with prominent **basalt columns** (see p91). A short distance OR to the W, there is a viewpoint overlooking **Markarfljótsgljúfur Canyon**. To continue on **Stage 4a**, TR and descend SE. At the base of the slope, ford a stream on rocks. Then head E across a basalt plain. Later, the path turns left, descending towards the **Fremri-Emstruá River**. Soon, the path becomes very exposed: there are chains bolted into the rock for safety.

2 5:20: Cross a bridge over a gorge: given the huge volume of water being forced down the chasm, this is a thrilling and noisy experience. On the far side, steps and a steep path lead upwards: there are ropes/handrails for safety. Soon, take care climbing a steep, sandy slope.

1 5:40: At the top of the slope, continue N on a path across more plains. After 15-20min, cross a footbridge over a stream. 10min later, after an **information board**, descend W into a narrow valley. Cross a stream, pass some tent pitches and climb the other side of the valley.

S 6:10: Arrive at **Emstrur/Botnar Hut (465m)**.

N-S see map on p96

Stage v4b: Húsadalur north exit to Húsadalur

30min; 1.7km; 14m/100m ascent/descent

From **F**, head initially SW on a path ('Húsadalur'). At any junctions, take the more northerly path and work your way generally W all the way to **Volcano Huts** at **Húsadalur**.

Stage v4c: Húsadalur to Þórsmörk (Langidalur)

30min; 1.7km; 60m/40m ascent/descent

From **Húsadalur**, head E on a path: ignore offshoots heading S. After 5-10min, TR at a junction and climb SE: at any junctions, head SE. Then at **1**, keep SH ('Þórsmörk'). 10min later, reach **Langidalur Hut**.

S-N see map on p96

Stage v4c: Þórsmörk (Langidalur) to Húsadalur

30min; 1.7km; 40m/60m ascent/descent

From **Langidalur Hut**, head N on a path. 10-15min later, keep SH at **1** ('Húsadalur'). At any junctions, head NW. 10min from **1**, the path bends left: head W all the way to **Húsadalur**.

Stage v4b: Húsadalur to Húsadalur north exit

35min; 1.7km; 100m/14m ascent/descent

From **Húsadalur**, walk E on a path (ignoring offshoots heading S). After 5-10min, TL at a junction and climb generally NE. Reach the **Húsadalur north exit** (**F**).

Emstrur/Botnar Hut

Fimmvörðuháls Trail

The Mýrdalsjökull glacier seen from the Morinsheiði Plateau (Stage 5b)

For many LT trekkers, the FT seems more like a continuation of the LT rather than a distinct trail with its own identity: this is not helped by the fact that many people try to avoid even saying the word *'Fimmvörðuháls'* because it is difficult to be sure how to pronounce it unless you speak Icelandic. However, the scenery of the FT is very different to that on the LT. Furthermore, the FT is harder than the LT and there are a number of reasons for this. Firstly, whichever direction you hike, the FT involves a long strenuous climb and a steep knee-jerking descent, both of which are much longer than any on the LT. Secondly, parts of the route (mainly on Stage 5b) are more steep and/or exposed than any terrain that the LT throws at you. Thirdly, route-finding can be more difficult than on the LT because bad weather, low visibility and snow make it difficult to navigate the more barren sections. And lastly, the spartan nature of the accommodation at the two small huts on the Fimmvörðuháls pass, and the lack of available drinking water there, mean that many people aim to complete the FT over one long day and that is a challenging proposition.

However, despite the difficulties, a great many trekkers maintain that the FT is the highlight of their trip to Iceland. The terrain is wonderfully varied with green slopes covered with shrubs and wild-flowers, barren deserts coated with ash from the 2010 eruption of Eyjafjallajökull, incredible lava flows, and lots of waterfalls. The FT is a raw and exciting way to start or finish your trek.

Fimmvörðuháls Trail: Þórsmörk-Langidalur/ Fimmvörðuháls exit

5

Whichever your direction of travel, Section 5 is the most challenging part of the LT/FT. However, your effort will be richly rewarded because it is also one of the most spectacular and exhilarating parts of the trek. You will climb/descend along a stunning knife-edge ridge with sheer drops and wide-ranging views over the green and fertile slopes on both sides of the Krossá River. However, at higher altitudes, the vegetation gives way to volcanic rock and ash and two active volcanoes dominate your attention: to the E, Katla which is capped with the vast Mýrdalsjökull Glacier and, to the W, the infamous Eyjafjallajökull which erupted in 2010 causing disruption all over Europe. The Fimmvörðuháls pass actually leads you through the gap between the two volcanoes which is a fascinating and sobering experience: everywhere you look, the eruption's devastating impact on the landscape is visible. The slopes are thickly coated with ash and other volcanic debris and, at Goðahraun, you actually walk across a huge lava flow and pass the two massive craters created during the effusive stages of the eruption. Snow lies at the pass throughout the year and it can be a cold and foreboding place: however, it is certainly atmospheric and quite unlike anything you will have experienced before.

Those intending to stay at the Fimmvörðuháls Hut (a.k.a. Fimmvörðuskáli Hut) should bear in mind that the hut is actually 20min OR from the Fimmvörðuháls exit at the S end of Stage 5b. The facilities are very basic: the kitchen, dining area and beds are all in one room so it is a tight squeeze. Each bed is shared by two people. In our opinion, Baldvinsskáli Hut, which is only 1.4km further S from the Fimmvörðuháls exit (along Stage 6a), is a more pleasant place to stay: see Section 6.

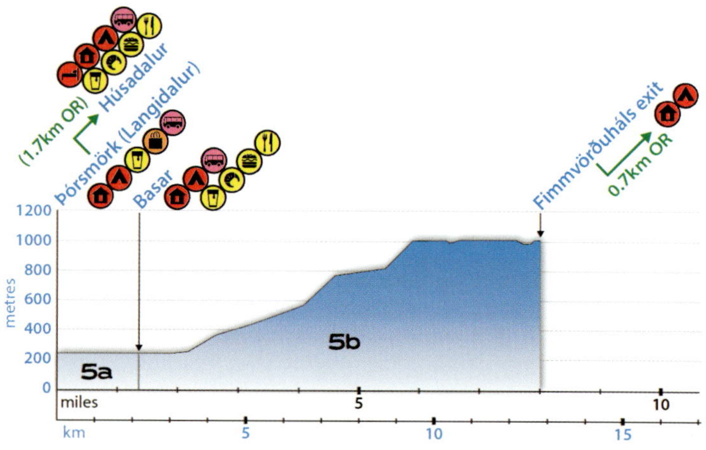

Neither hut has a source of drinking water: the hut managers often melt a little snow which you could drink after treatment but, as that is not a very appealing prospect, most trekkers carry their own drinking water up with them. For S-N trekkers, this is not a big problem because plenty of water is available from the river not too far from Baldvinsskáli Hut. However, N-S trekkers will have to carry water all the way up from the bottom of the climb at Básar.

On paper, the short, flat Stage 5a looks straightforward but in practice, it is not so easy because the rocky bed of the Krossá River is hard to walk upon. The navigation posts are difficult to follow too, making the mobile bridge across the main channel of the river hard to locate, particularly in low visibility: if in doubt, head SE. Although you may have to ford some smaller channels of the river, do not attempt to cross the main channel without using the bridge: the water is deep and powerful. Because the bridge is mobile, it may in fact be located upstream or downstream of the position indicated on the map: the posts should guide you towards its general location.

Stage 5b is a high-altitude route and you should not attempt it in poor conditions or low visibility when navigation on certain sections can be tricky. Route-finding N of ❷ is generally straightforward because the paths are mostly clearly defined and there are frequent wooden posts for guidance. However, S of ❷, navigation is more difficult: on the flat Morinsheiði Plateau, for example, it is easy to get disorientated in low visibility. Furthermore, large parts of the route are frequently snow-covered, particularly S of ❸, making route-finding more difficult. Always remain on the path (if any) and follow blue or yellow markers carefully.

Parts of Stage 5b are steep and/or unstable. Occasionally, the drops are sheer and a fall could be serious: tread carefully and make use of any fixed ropes/chains. Take particular care negotiating the exposed rock outcrop near ❸: always wait for others to finish before starting across the narrow sections protected with fixed chains/ropes. Stage 5b is not suitable for those with a fear of heights.

Buses to/from Reykjavík stop at Básar (Stage 5a/5b), Langidalur (Stage 4b/5a) and Húsadalur (Stage v4b/v4c: 1.7km OR).

		Time	Distance	Ascent N-S	Descent N-S
Stage 5a	Þórsmörk-Langidalur/Básar	0:30	2.2km 1.4miles	0m 0ft	0m 0ft
Stage 5b	Básar/Fimmvörðuháls exit	5:15(N-S) 4:00(S-N)	10.7km 6.7miles	977m 3206ft	192m 630ft

Accommodation

▶ **Langidalur Hut at Þórsmörk (Stage 4b/5a):** 75 dormitory beds; kitchen with gas stoves/utensils; toilets; showers

▶ **Básar Mountain Hut (Stage 5a/5b):** 83 dormitory beds; kitchen with gas stoves/utensils; toilets; showers

▶ **Fimmvörðuháls/Fimmvörðuskáli Hut (Stage 5b/6a; 0.7km OR):** 23 spaces on shared beds; kitchen with gas stoves/utensils; toilet; no showers; no running water

Camping

▶ **Langidalur Hut at Þórsmörk (Stage 4b/5a):** grassy, sloping campsite beside the hut

▶ **Básar (Stage 5a/5b):** the sprawling campsite can get quite busy with locals in the summer. The most peaceful pitches are near the bridge (further E): the toilet block here is beside the start of the Stage 5b climb and is a good place to top up water bottles

► **Fimmvörðuháls/Fimmvörðuskáli Hut (Stage 5b/6a; 0.7km OR):** you can camp on the volcanic rock beside the hut but this can be a brutally cold and windy place. Place rocks on top of pegs to prevent your tent from blowing away

Refreshments/Food

► **Básar (Stage 5a/5b):** small restaurant/bar

Supplies

► **Langidalur Hut at Þórsmörk (Stage 4b/5a):** basic shop (snacks/drinks/freeze-dried meals/gas)

Escape/Access

► **Langidalur Hut at Þórsmörk (Stage 4b/5a):** bus
► **Básar (Stage 5a/5b):** bus

Krossá River

Hrunag
Hrun
Morinsheiði
Gljúfragil
2
3
Heljarkambur (793m)
4
Memorial
5
Móði (1130m)
Magni (1165m)
Stage 5b
rtungnahaus (868m)
Úthólmar
Goðahraun
Brattafönn
jökull
H r
Miðsker
Austurgígar
Fimmvörðuháls/
Fimmvörðuskáli Hut
(1030m)
Fimmvörðusker
9
F S
Fimmvörðuháls
Fimmvörðuháls
Stage 6a
Baldvinsskáli Hut
(905m)
F
S
10
Stage 6b
Landnorðurstungur
Slæðufoss

These two craters within the **Goðahraun lava field** were formed during the 2010 eruptions of **Eyjafjallajökull**. The first eruption, which began on 20 March 2010, was an effusive one: it opened a 300m fissure on the **Fimmvörðuháls pass**. At a certain stage during this eruption, the activity exclusively occurred at a single point on the fissure: this formed the crater, **Magni**. On 31 March, another fissure opened which intersected the first one: it created **Móði**. When the effusive eruption from the fissures ended in April, the heights of Magni and Móði were 82m and 47m respectively. The Goðahraun lava field is 10-20m thick and has a surface area of 1.2 km².

Fimmvörðuháls/Fimmvörðuskáli Hut Side-trip

20min (one way); 0.7km (one way); 40m ascent/descent

From the junction (**F**), head W along a ridge, following posts: the path is faint and uneven. Soon, the path bends right, descending steeply over banks of ash. At the bottom, there are two options. Firstly, you could cross the stream and head directly up the steep crest of the ridge which will lead to the hut. However, the main route skirts to the right of the ridge and follows the N bank of the stream. After 5min, TL and cross the stream. Then climb steeply up the slopes of ash, following posts. TR at the crest of the ridge and follow it all the way to **Fimmvörðuháls/Fimmvörðuskáli Hut (1030m)**. The small building occupies a barren windswept spot on top of the ridge, a short distance from **Eyjafjallajökull's ice-cap**. We have tried both options and are not convinced that the main route is much better than the direct route: both are steep and occasionally unstable, requiring the use of your hands. To continue on the FT, retrace your steps back to **F**.

Rauði
(801m)

Stage 5a: Þórsmörk (Langidalur) to Básar

S From the warden's hut, head E along the bank of the **Krossá River**. After a few minutes, TR, crossing a pair of streams. Then head SE, following posts across the rubble of the broad riverbed. You may have to ford some small channels of the river.

1 0:25: TR and cross the main channel using a mobile bridge. Because the bridge is mobile, the location changes slightly but the posts should lead you close to it. After crossing, follow posts to an access road: TL and enter the campsite.

F 0:30: Reach a junction at the **Básar Campsite information office**. TL on a path to look for camping pitches or to start **Stage 5b**. Alternatively, keep SH to head to **Básar Hut**.

Stage 5b: Básar to Fimmvörðuháls exit

S From the **campsite information office**, head E through the campsite, following marker posts. 10min later, cross a footbridge and TL. Shortly afterwards, pass a toilet block: you can top up your water bottles.

1 0:15: Shortly afterwards, TR on a path (easy to miss). From here, you will be climbing all the way to the Fimmvörðuháls pass. Stay on the main path, ignoring offshoots: follow marker posts. Initially, the path climbs through vegetation up the NE side of the steep-edged **Strákagil Valley**: sometimes, the route is steep and exposed. Pass along a knife-edge ridge with sheer drops on either side (**Kattarhryggir**): at one point there is a fixed chain for safety. As you climb higher, there are some exquisite viewpoints.

2 2:40: Head S across the broad, stony **Morinsheiði Plateau**, covered with rock from the 2010 eruption: follow marker posts carefully in low visibility. Soon, keep SH at a junction.

3 3:15: At a signpost near the edge of cliffs, TR and descend steeply over rocks. At a saddle, keep SH, climbing steeply. Soon, bear right at an outcrop and use fixed chains to traverse the exposed W side of it: take care as the drops are steep. In fact, some people climb straight up the steep face of the outcrop instead of skirting to the W of it, but we would not recommend this. Soon, TL and climb steeply between rocks: there are more chains to assist but be careful as they are not always firmly affixed. Afterwards, follow yellow posts up the steep slope.

4 4:05: The gradient levels.

5 4:10: TL at a fork, following yellow markers SW across the **Goðahraun lava field**: be aware that the path heading right from the fork also has identical yellow markers. Often the ground is covered with snow and the lava field can be a disorientating place. Soon pass **Magni** and **Móði**, two craters which formed during the 2010 eruption (see p107): if you have the energy, there are paths to the summits of both craters.

F 5:15: Shortly after passing a signpost (marking the highest point on the broad **Fimmvörðuháls pass**), reach a junction. Keep SH for **Stage 6a** to **Baldvinsskáli Hut** or TR for the **Fimmvörðuháls/Fimmvörðuskáli Hut Side-trip** (see p107).

Stage 5b: Fimmvörðuháls exit to Básar

F From the junction, head N. Soon cross the highest point on the broad **Fimmvörðuháls pass**. After a broad plateau, follow yellow markers N across the **Goðahraun lava field**. Soon pass **Magni** and **Móði**, two craters which formed during the 2010 eruption (see p107): if you have the energy, there are paths to the summits of both craters.

5 0:50: Keep SH at a junction.

4 0:55: Descend N on a steep, unstable path, following yellow posts. Reach the top of a steep outcrop: some people climb straight down the outcrop but we do not recommend this. TL and descend steeply between rocks: there are chains to assist but be careful because they are not always firmly affixed. Soon, bear right and use fixed chains to traverse the exposed W side of the outcrop: take care as the drops are steep. Keep SH across a saddle and then climb steeply through rocks.

3 1:35: At the top of the slope, TL at a signpost and head N across the broad, stony **Morinsheiði Plateau** which is covered with rock from the 2010 eruption: follow marker posts carefully in low visibility.

2 2:10: Descend to the N. Soon follow posts along the crest of a ridge. Later, the ridge (**Kattarhryggir**) becomes very narrow, with sheer drops on either side: at one point, there is a fixed chain for safety. Eventually, the path descends the NE side of the steep-edged **Strákagil Valley**: in places, the route is exposed. Stay on the main path, ignoring offshoots: follow marker posts.

1 3:45: TL at a junction near a stream. Shortly afterwards, TR and cross a footbridge. Head W through **Básar Campsite**, following marker posts.

S 4:00: Reach a junction at the **Básar Campsite information office**. TR on the access road for Stage 5a or TL for **Básar Hut**.

Stage 5a: Básar to Þórsmörk (Langidalur)

F From the **campsite information office**, head NW on the access road. Near the entrance to the campsite, TR and follow posts to the rocky bed of the **Krossá River**. Then head for a mobile bridge (on wheels) which you should hopefully see somewhere nearby: because the bridge is mobile, the location changes slightly but the posts should lead you close to it.

1 0:05: Cross the river using the mobile bridge. Then head NW, following posts across the rubble of the broad riverbed. You may have to ford some small channels of the river. Just before reaching the N bank of the river, cross a pair of streams. Then TL and head W along the bank.

S 0:30: Arrive at **Langidalur Hut (225m)**.

The bleak approach to Fimmvörðuháls Hut

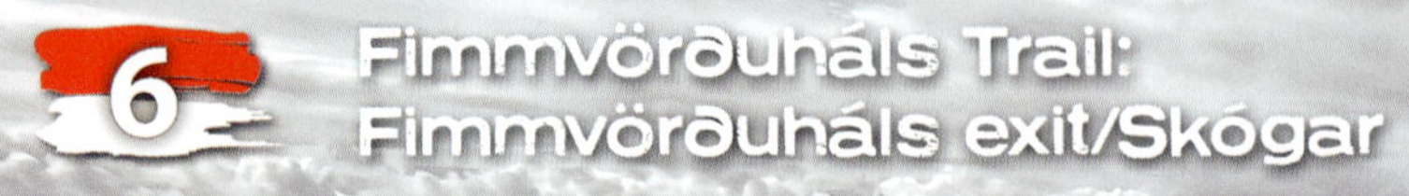

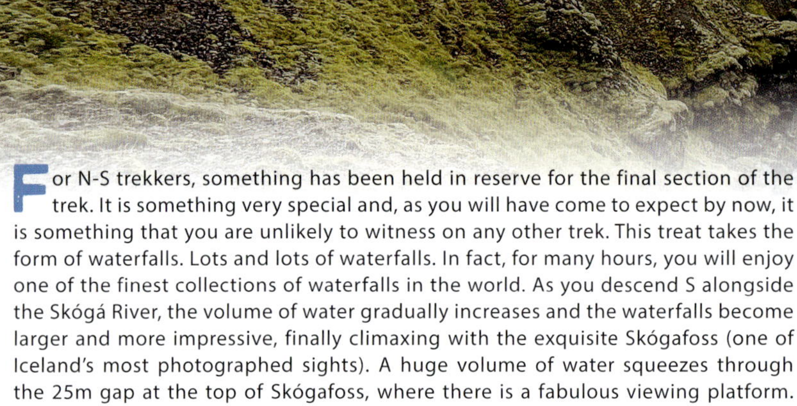

or N-S trekkers, something has been held in reserve for the final section of the trek. It is something very special and, as you will have come to expect by now, it is something that you are unlikely to witness on any other trek. This treat takes the form of waterfalls. Lots and lots of waterfalls. In fact, for many hours, you will enjoy one of the finest collections of waterfalls in the world. As you descend S alongside the Skógá River, the volume of water gradually increases and the waterfalls become larger and more impressive, finally climaxing with the exquisite Skógafoss (one of Iceland's most photographed sights). A huge volume of water squeezes through the 25m gap at the top of Skógafoss, where there is a fabulous viewing platform. The base of the falls is 62m below and, if you get too close to it, you will be soaked by the spray which often produces a beautiful rainbow. For S-N trekkers, heading upstream, the volume of water in the river gradually reduces but the display is still incredibly impressive. In almost any other place, each of the waterfalls, on its own, would be the centre of attention.

1.4km S of the Fimmvörðuháls exit, along Stage 6a, there is accommodation at Baldvinsskáli Hut. In our opinion, it is a more pleasant place to stay than the Fimmvörðuháls Hut (further N) and it actually lies on the FT route, whereas the Fimmvörðuháls Hut is 20min OR. Neither hut has a source of drinking water. For further information, see p102.

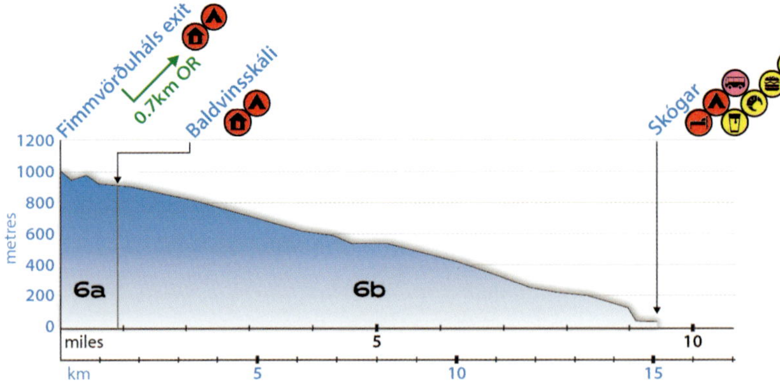

Skógar, at the S end of the FT, is a pleasant place although It Is very busy with day-trippers. The campsite has both positive and negative attributes: on the one hand, it is close to the magnificent Skógafoss so you can enjoy it late into the evening when it is more peaceful. On the other hand, the campsite is also located beside the waterfall's busy car park and is not a particularly relaxing place during the day. However, with the waterfall, Skógar Museum and the good restaurant/bar at Hotel Skógafoss, there is plenty to keep you away from your tent until the evening, when most of the day-trippers have departed. Hotel Skógafoss is a comfortable place to stay but you will need to book well in advance in peak season. There used to be a youth hostel but sadly, this has closed permanently.

For N-S trekkers, Section 6 is much easier than Section 5: the route is mostly downhill and makes use of many clear tracks/paths. S-N trekkers, of course, will have to endure a long climb but this is made easier by the frequent breaks you will take as you gaze at the waterfalls. Take care on Stage 6a's steep ash slopes which are frequently snow-covered and can be slippery: follow marker posts carefully to avoid drifting OR. Otherwise, navigation is usually straightforward.

The last bus to Reykjavík leaves Skógar in the middle of the afternoon so N-S trekkers who overnight at Fimmvörðuháls/Baldvinsskáli should not need to rush Section 6: it will probably be too cold near the pass to sleep in late anyway! The bus stop is beside Hotel Skógafoss. If you are hiking the entire FT in one day, then you are unlikely to arrive in Skógar before the last bus departs and will have to spend the night there.

		Time	Distance	Ascent N-S	Descent N-S
Stage 6a	Fimmvörðuháls exit/Baldvinsskáli	0:30(N-S) 0:45(S-N)	1.4km 0.9miles	35m 115ft	140m 459ft
Stage 6b	Baldvinsskáli/ Skógar	4:00(N-S) 5:30(S-N)	13.7km 8.5miles	122m 400ft	1002m 3288ft

Accommodation

▶ **Fimmvörðuháls/Fimmvörðuskáli Hut (Stage 5b/6a; 0.7km OR):** 23 spaces on shared beds; kitchen with gas stoves/utensils; toilet; no showers; no running water

▶ **Baldvinsskáli Hut (Stage 6a/6b):** 16 sleeping spaces; kitchen with gas stoves/utensils; toilet; no showers; no running water

▶ **Skógar (Stage 6b):** Hotel Skógafoss; the hostel has closed permanently

Camping

▶ **Fimmvörðuháls/Fimmvörðuskáli Hut (Stage 5b/6a; 0.7km OR):** you can camp on the volcanic rock beside the hut but this can be a brutally cold and windy place. Place rocks on top of pegs to prevent your tent from blowing away

▶ **Baldvinsskáli Hut (Stage 6a/6b):** you can camp on the volcanic rock beside the hut but this can be a brutally cold and windy place. Place rocks on top of pegs to prevent your tent from blowing away

The Skógafoss Legend

According to legend, around 900 CE, an early Viking settler (who was a sorcerer) buried a chest filled with gold behind Skógafoss. In 1600, three men tried to remove the chest from behind the waterfall by pulling on a gold ring on the side of it: the ring broke and the chest was lost. The ring is on display in Skógar Museum.

► **Skógar (Stage 6b):** the campsite is the grassy area at the Skógafoss car park. There is a toilet/shower block nearby

Refreshments/Food
► **Skógar (Stage 6b):** Hotel Skógafoss Bistro Bar (breakfast/lunch/dinner; open to non-residents); Mia's Country Van Fish & Chips (takeaway); Café Skógar at Skógar Museum

Supplies
► None

Escape/Access
► **Skógar (Stage 6b):** bus

Skógafoss is one of Iceland's top attractions

Slæðufoss
Miðfoss (25m high)
& Neðstifoss
Neðstifoss
Miðfoss
Efstif
Fimm
1
Grængil
Skógafoss
Skógá
Hornfellsnípa
Fimmvörðuháls
Stage 6b
Króksfoss
Skó
Innribotnar
Rollutorfufoss
(5m high/37m wide)
Krókur
Kæfufoss
(14m high/25-35m wide)
nau
Gluggafoss
Fremri-Botnar
Dal
Drang
Kæfufoss
Skálabrekkur
Skálabrekkufoss
Fimmvörðuháls
Rollutorfufoss
Hrútafellsheiði
Innri-Fellsfoss
Laufatungur
Fremri-Fellsfoss
Þvergil
Stígagil
Steinbogafoss
Selvaðsfoss
Stage 6b
Runsugil
Selfoss
Skógagil
Fosstorfufoss
Yxnadalur
Skógafoss
Hestavaðsfoss
Hestavaðsfoss (9m high)
íðarfjall
2
11
K
Kver
Drangshlíðardal
Skógar
F
12
Skógasafn
Skógar Museum
Skógavegur
-Skógavegur
Suður

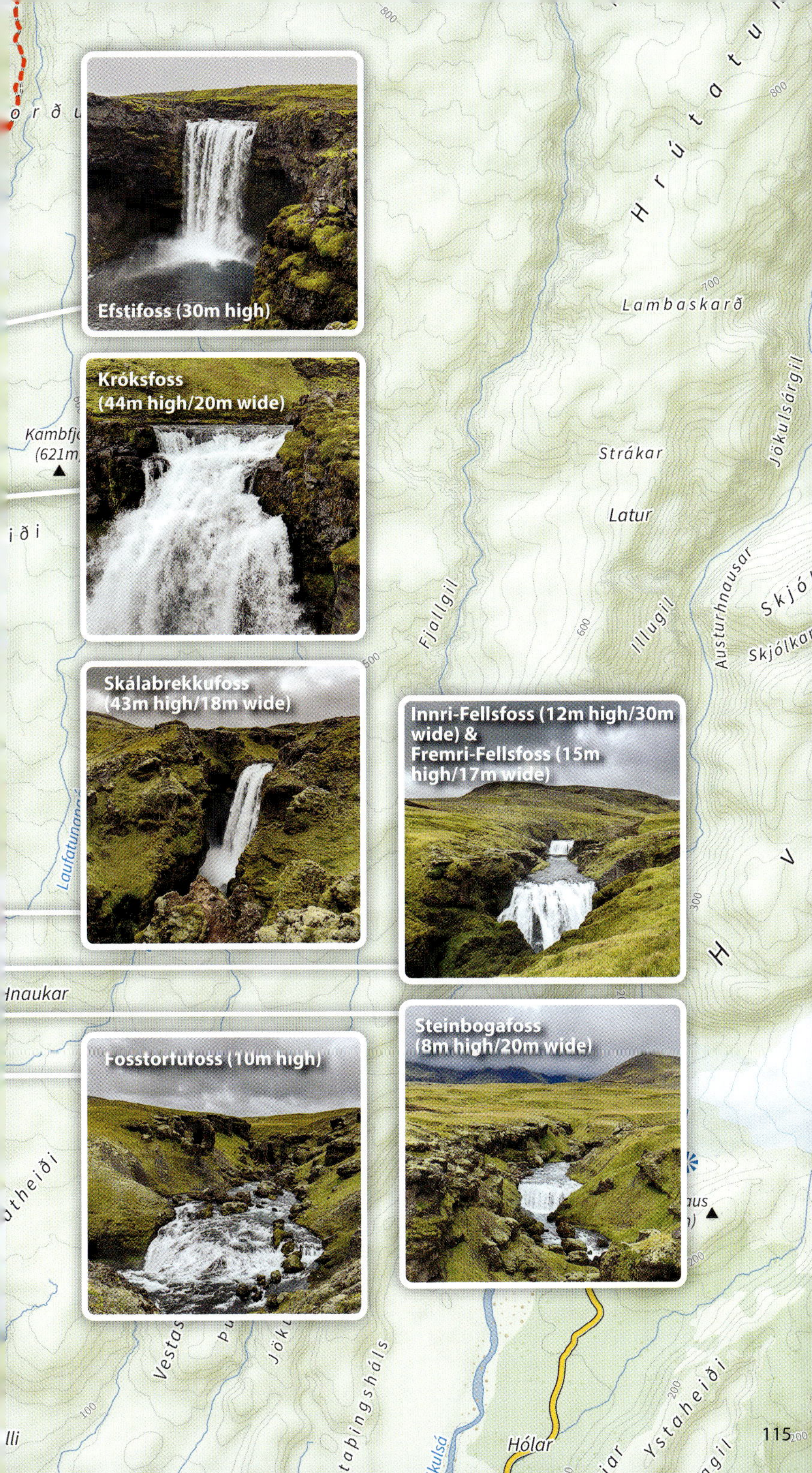
800
Hrútatu
Lambaskarð
700
Jökulsárgil
Strákar
Latur
Kambfj
(621m
Austurhnausar
Skjól
Skjólkar
Fjallgil
Illugil
iði
600
500
Hnaukar
Laufatunang
V
H
300
Innri-Fellsfoss (12m high/30m wide) &
Fremri-Fellsfoss (15m high/17m wide)
Skálabrekkufoss
(43m high/18m wide)
Króksfoss
(44m high/20m wide)
Efstifoss (30m high)
Fosstorfufoss (10m high)
Steinbogafoss
(8m high/20m wide)
utheiði
jus
)
200
Vestas
Jökul
Pu
tabingsháls
lli
Vestari
Ystaheiði
100
200
200
Jökulsá
Hólar
agil
115

N-S see map on p106

Stage 6a: Fimmvörðuháls exit to Baldvinsskáli

S From the junction, continue S across the ash-covered slopes. For now, the path undulates: it is steep and the remaining snow/ice can be slippery (especially on cold mornings). Follow yellow posts carefully. Soon, the path descends more steadily.

F 0:30: Reach **Baldvinsskáli Hut (905m)**.

Stage 6b: Baldvinsskáli to Skógar

S From **Baldvinsskáli Hut**, descend on a track (marker posts). The terrain gradually becomes greener and more welcoming. After a while, you will reach the first of Stage 6b's waterfalls: even these smaller ones are impressive.

1 1:20: TL at a signpost (which is slightly misleading). Shortly afterwards, cross a footbridge over the river. Then TR and head SW along the riverbank. From now to the end of the stage, you will pass a series of amazing waterfalls and your progress will slow substantially. The path is usually simple to follow but occasionally, it disappears across rocky ground: follow posts carefully and do not drift too far from the **Skógá River**.

2 3:50: Reach a **viewing platform** at the top of **Skógafoss**, the largest and most spectacular of Stage 6b's waterfalls. The view is amazing but the crowds of people will be a shock to the system after so many days of tranquillity. Descend steps to arrive near the base of the waterfall: you can walk closer to it but the spray will soak you. Continue S through the **campsite/car park**.

F 4:00: Arrive at the **bus stop** in **Skógar** (beside **Hotel Skógafoss**).

S-N see map on p114

Stage 6b: Skógar to Baldvinsskáli

F From the **bus stop** beside **Hotel Skógafoss**, head N through the **campsite/car park**. Arrive near the base of **Skógafoss**, the largest and most spectacular of Stage 6b's waterfalls: if you get too close, you will be soaked by spray. Climb steps.

2 0:15: Reach an amazing **viewing platform** at the top of the waterfall. Follow a path which climbs N alongside the **Skógá River**. For the next few hours, you will pass a series of amazing waterfalls and your progress will be slow. The path is usually simple to follow but occasionally, it disappears across rocky ground: follow posts carefully and do not drift too far from the river.

1 3:45: Cross a footbridge over the river. Shortly afterwards, TR at a signpost and continue N along the W side of the river.

S 5:30: Reach **Baldvinsskáli Hut (905m)**.

Stage 6a: Baldvinsskáli to Fimmvörðuháls exit

F From **Baldvinsskáli Hut**, head N on a path which soon climbs steadily. Later, the gradient increases as you climb the ash-covered slopes.

S 0:45: Reach a junction. Keep SH for Stage 5b to **Básar** or TL for the side-trip to **Fimmvörðuháls/Fimmvörðuskáli Hut** (see p107).